Liberating Love

Liberating Love

The Impact of Culture, History, and Economics
On the Traditional Ideals of Intimacy

Paul Dennis Sporer

QUENSTEDT PRESS

ANZA PUBLISHING, Chester, New York
Quenstedt Press is an imprint of Anza Publishing
Copyright © 2010 by Paul Dennis Sporer

Library of Congress Cataloguing-in-Publication Data
Sporer, Paul D.
   Liberating love / Paul Dennis Sporer.
      p. cm.
   Includes bibliographical references and index.
   ISBN–13: 978–1–932490–33–6 (softcover : alk. paper)
   ISBN-10: 1–932490–33–7 (softcover : alk. paper)
   1. Love.
   2. Marriage.
   3. Liberty.
   4. Man-woman relationships.
   I. Title.
BF575.L8S644 2008
177'.7--dc22   2008013406

Visit AnzaPublishing.com for more information on outstanding
authors and titles. Please support our efforts to restore great
literature to a place of prominence in our culture.

ISBN-13: 978–1–932490–33–6 (softcover)

∞ This book is printed on acid-free paper.

To my dearest Cassandra

CONTENTS

Chapter 1

Introduction

*L*iberty, independence, freedom—we hear these words frequently from earliest childhood, spoken often with great seriousness and intonation. Being without restraint indeed strikes a unique, almost ineffable impression on the mind. Like a free-fall, liberty can feel like an intoxicating rush. Doing exactly what one wants, and not having to obey rules about what to think, what to do, what to say, where to go, what to wear—these are the things that humans innately seek. The release from a dreary obligation creates an extraordinary moment, most potent while still in the full memory of what has transpired. Whether it is travelling on a journey, learning a new language, moving into a new home, or becoming the owner of a business—whatever the level of complexity—the casting off of shackles can be exhilarating. For young people about to enter adulthood, the mind reels at the tremendous possibilities that independence finally bestows. Truly, the struggle for freedom involves all ages and backgrounds. Social leaders and government officials frequently claim that 'liberty' is the most precious harvest of democratic participation. Yet the word 'liberty' and its synonyms, when given fullest expression, are proud, bold, defiant; they imply an attitude that devalues, even discards, fellowship and mutualism as a means of fulfilment. Nonetheless, the exercise of independence does not have to be selfish, if one uses it only to attain control over life. Once ability and strength are allied with compassion, then the ideal of love can be developed.

Love—a word that can also conjure up great emotion, but one that quite frankly wavers when confronted with 'emancipation' and 'free choice'. Love invariably involves being dependent to some extent on someone else, and that creates a challenge to the concept of independence. However, no matter how much one has basked in the glory of cutting bindings from oneself, the shadow of emotional desire, of affection, can never be left behind. Western cultures have repeatedly made it clear that, we cannot experience total fulfilment in life unless there is also love. In a modern world that promotes and rewards autonomy, freedom can come cheaply, yet love then comes at a premium, because the bold concept of independence comes at the risk of injury to the most crucial dynamic in a relationship, the spirit of cooperation.

Today, society makes onerous demands on people, where there is a cost not only to individual well-being, but to social stability as well. To counteract the anxious tidal forces brought on by independent minds each pulling their own way, companionship is more necessary than ever. The solidity of two people in a deep affectionate embrace can overcome all waves of change. But love cannot flourish where people press for self-determination; it is hard to strike a balance since, compared to love, the costs of independence are relatively inexpensive, and the returns are immediate.

Are love and independence implacable foes?

From the dream-like world of childhood, autonomy rises up as one of our great primary visions. Love is usually taken for granted, unless it is withheld by guardians, relatives and others in one's social circle. It occurs naturally, as simple a concept as independence, but always strongly prone to subjective emotional forces. Quite in contrast, independence revolves around material questions and factors, which appear in various guises at different psychological phases. The desire for freedom grows out of the failure to satisfy basic personal needs. We would not need to discuss the concept of independence, if we could always find easy success in our endeavours. When we say, one has obtained 'freedom' from something, that something must have made significant impositions on one's time, resources, intellect and emotions. The sequence of liberation is often the same: The first freedom is from the household of childhood, the second from school and teachers, the third is from an occupation, the fourth is from community and institutions. Thus, autonomy is a relative concept, entangled in context, dependent on other questions that are pertinent, such as happiness, security, friendship, mature love, self-respect, equality, comfort, and accomplishment. Love, on the other hand, stands alone, being contingent on the interaction between only two people.

It does not take long before the maturing individual discovers that life always demands a combination of freedom and service. A key question is often asked: How much freedom can an individual give up, and still be 'free'? It is not only a case of striking a balance between the two, but using each wisely. Everyone wants to be free to *choose* their own destiny, but the life one freely chooses might not be free of constraint. A person might choose to work in service to someone else, leaving hardly any time for self-directed activities. The choice of becoming a servant was entirely his, but after this free exercise of choice, the rest of life is largely given over to the decisions of his superior. This individual is indeed 'free', if by this decision he is able to avoid worry, self-doubt and conceit. He might be able to achieve all the respect and appreciation he wants in this lifestyle, in spite of the criticisms and ridicule of others about his 'despised' state. Hence, one can be truly free, and still sacrifice for another, if that is his choice. The *context* of the situation must, therefore, always be borne in mind.

However, there is no guarantee that the individual will develop the concept of 'liberty' or 'love' as an integrated whole. Instead, human beings tend to focus their attention on *results*, such as contentment, more than *methods*, such as democracy, equality, culture, solidarity, marriage, or free enterprise. Consequently, when asked directly, 'What is the most important goal in life?', the consensus is overwhelming: *Happiness*. Nevertheless, the young person might only have a hazy conception as to how to achieve this goal, and only with age does he or she develop the knowledge to understand the method to deliver the result. Thus, in a survey of young people, 'happiness' was put ahead of 'freedom' or 'love', but in a survey consisting mostly of adults, 'family' was put first, then 'freedom'.[1] For adults, freedom is *not* the end result in life, but only a *means* to achieve something that is highly important, that of family. However, we cannot easily separate happiness, family, love, and freedom, as they are all are interrelated concepts. Clearly, each component has its own rewards, but freedom and family can also be methods to fulfill the other two (love and happiness). Accordingly, if we are properly to examine the issue of independence, we must recognise that most people see it as being of secondary importance, perhaps only a means to an end. Love is a more complex issue to resolve, being found in many different situations, and so resists easy prioritisation.

Concepts relating to affection usually arise from a realisation of the coldness and sterility of autonomy. Love develops as needs become complex, as the individual becomes vulnerable and understands he cannot go it alone. One has no problem accepting the advantages of affection, but one must initially determine the costs linked to independence. Ideally, there would be little or no cost, but this is highly unusual. More likely, love takes a significant portion of one's freedom. Yet, we should also see that a loss of freedom due to other reasons can be compensated for by love. People sometimes do so successfully, but as love is the superior dynamic, it does not work the other way around, that is, freedom cannot make up for a deficiency of affection. People living in countries disrupted by dehumanising systems of government, or by the violence of war experience less freedom, and so are more likely to desire companionship as compensation. Perhaps this is the reason why people in some areas of the world are more strongly in favour of marriage than in other areas.[2]

More than just temporary affection is needed, however, for the individual to feel *fulfilled*. The affection must last a lifetime, and indeed, from the individual's perspective, it must be *eternal*. There is no doubt that, as all things pass in this world, and in order for love to be transcendent, it must be *different* in substantive ways from all other artefacts of existence. This means that two people must *intend* that the mutually respectful attachment between them will always endure, even though the possibility always remains. In other words, a husband and wife must have *absolute* faith that their love for one another will never end, no matter what circumstances appertain. If there is even the slightest doubt that the consideration will end, then it is *not* true love. Such statements appear harsh, but, as the objective person understands, we have no control over the rules of the real world, we can only observe and respect them.

Thus, the basis of love is the desire for an exceptional friendship. Friendships are formed naturally and easily, often without much thought behind the process. Note the causal sequence: There must be a friendship before there can be love, but love does not necessarily arise from a friendship. The relationship which is uppermost in the minds of everyone is the unique bond, a genuinely mature union that can only exist between a man and a woman. True love, which is to say lasting love, can mutually occur between any two people, but it is most keenly felt and most extensive when it is between a man and woman, because each possesses what the other desires in order to be complete and perfect.

We should not underestimate the power of this relationship. Despite the rush of mundane business, in the midst of all the commotion and clatter of worldly matters, the allure of the opposite sex never seems to falter. Hence, no matter where a man or woman finds himself or herself, even in isolation, even where the sexes are in a great imbalance and a mate can be found only with difficulty, the conception faithfully, perhaps irrationally, lives on. With grow-ing maturity, one realises the uniqueness of a male-female friend-ship, and one understands that it can transcend all common or conventional facets of life. Work, school, the neighbourhood, rela-tives, obligations to company, family, state, and church, can all be places where this relationship begins, but *genuine intimate friend-ship* will always outgrow the place where it began. Nothing can ultimately keep it from growing, and nothing can ever ruin it. The only end to the true love between a man and woman must come from the inside, not the outside. And, of course, if a supposedly true love relationship ends, then it was not true love to begin with. The test of a friendship is its ability to resist to threats and stresses; it must be profound and long-lasting.

Where do we find true friendship? We find it through observing behaviour which will lead to mutual respect; without respect there is no trust, and therefore no exchange of knowledge, resources, and validation. *Respect* is ultimately built on the belief that the other person has *control over his or her life,* derived from rational, thoughtful behaviour, and allied with compassion and concern. Further, one can learn from the other how to be in control, because respect breeds a desire to imitate the best characteristics of the other. Respect is a highly significant fundamental concept where the binding effects act in a recursive fashion. Hence, if a wife says 'my husband does not listen to me', we can gather much from this simple statement. We know that she and he are both not in control; she is not, because the husband does not respect her, and he is not, because she has not at least learned from her husband how to be in control. Conscious regulation of various areas is essential, and this ability is manifested in one's traits.

Clearly, in searching out friendship, there are many personal characteristics that emerge from one's background and personality, literally hundreds of details relating to emotions, intellect, phy-sique, career, education, and habits can be subsumed into categories. We can fortunately say that aspects exist which are universally attractive, and that are objectively superior to other attributes. These traits are called *virtues*—a word derived from the Latin *virtus* meaning *strength*—because they bestow power on the individual who possesses them. The virtuous person is worthy of esteem, and it can come from his own family, friends, or even further afield. The virtues are described using many different terms, often depending on whether the discourse is considered religious or secular. They can, however, be distilled to seven essential concepts (although these are not exhaustive descriptions):

❖ Purity: clarity of mind and healthiness of body; a resolve not to have one's intellect dulled by status pursuits, servitude to trends, or toxic ideas, or to have one's physical strength impaired by overindulgence in food, drink, or harmful substances.

❖ Objectivity: honesty; sincerity; a good faith investigation of a situation, and consideration of all the relevant facts.

❖ Perfectability: a need to eliminate all ignorance, all ugliness in character, and all wastefulness; a search for understanding; a desire to practise correctness in all situations; a strong desire for self-improvement.

❖ Caution (reservation, scepticism): a desire to carefully study and test all things, especially before a large investment of resources is made, so as to prevent neglect, exploitation or destruction.

❖ Devotion: the desire and discipline to hold on to what is good and to shun what is bad; a genuine preparation to make sacrifices and to renounce personal aims when necessary.

❖ Empathy: a habitual action where the individual puts himself in the place of others who might be affected by his behaviour, in order to vicariously experience their thoughts and feelings.

❖ Integrity: the ability to look at oneself as a complete individual, with a stable, integrated persona; the desire to maximise one's reputation, and the desire to see all the other virtues maximised and existing simultaneously.

Whatever way one cares to describe virtue—trust, dedication, cooperation, generosity, loyalty, truthfulness, purity of motive, confidence—all are approaches and attitudes that will yield the *best success*, no matter what the situation. Thus, the benefits of virtue are self-evident. Can anyone say that they find devotion or sincerity a negative trait, or selfishness or dishonesty a virtue? Can anyone say that one esteems liars, sycophants, cheats, layabouts or traitors? There might be people who cast some small regard upon those who do not conform to conventions, but this confraternity of iconoclasts is but weakly allied. The closest ties always rest upon the continual witnessing of highly regarded attributes.

Why are virtues so important in a relationship? The virtues reveal a love of oneself, a means for the individual to bring regulation over his life, through intelligent, constructive decisions that bring far more rewards than losses. Those who poison their minds and bodies, those who become involved in deceit, those who care only about short-term expediency, those who rush into making decisions in order to please or impress others, those who are not interested in the truth but only status—without exception such people make key mistakes that bring misery. How can one expect to have someone love them when they do not even love themselves? How can someone who acts self-destructively, that is, someone who treats himself with malevolence, be expected to treat someone else with kindness? How can someone who does not care to seek the best in himself, and in his own life, be expected to elicit what is best in someone else? When people possess the virtues, then and only then, can genuine love occur.

These fundamental good attitudes provide the engine for developing and grounding other ideas, pertaining to areas such as group dynamics, economy, education, social customs, and government. Simply put, material and social exigencies often clash with emotional and intellectual needs, and how a person resolves these conflicts in favour of a positive result for himself and others, is a measure of his character. Surety of similarity in views between two people of good moral character, although desirable, is not guaranteed, however. In the area of politics, for example, a person among whose virtues is honesty, believes that conservative parties can have a major impact on moral values, whereas another person of equal probity believes that they will have little influence. The fact that there is a divergence of opinion does not negate the fact that both people are upright, and so *potentially* true friends; because of their virtue, each gives his viewpoint sincerely, without concealed motive. Virtue acts as a reliable system, a dynamism, that produces other attitudes, an impetus for seeking rectitude in all areas of life. The fact that all such people of virtue do not agree might be due to differences in education, intelligence, perspective, or most likely, specificity. Misunderstandings can be remedied through gainful and honest discourse. Consequently, amongst people who possess virtue, and thus command respect, we can say that the major *fundamental* factors of belief will always be analogous, the *derived* factors might, or might not, be so. Further, high virtue does not necessarily mean possessing the same set of viewpoints, but it does mean responding in a similar fashion to the same situation.

It is essential that we stress the fact that, although allure for the *whole* person is what makes for true love, it is attraction for only *part* of a person that is common in modern society. Why should this be? Simply because one is more likely to favour one member, or a small number of members of a set, over most members of a set, other things being equal. Whereas most people will ignore, or even treat with suspicion, many of the traits a person possesses, they will find some level of attraction towards at least a few traits, and therefore, only a few traits constitute the person's image in the mind of the average person. Accordingly, attraction between the sexes is more likely to be a fascination with merely a subdivision of an individual's set of behaviours and attitudes, resulting in an inability to make sacrifices because respect has not been established.³ Those who do understand true love do not require any lessons, for the details come easily. But few are so endowed, and everyone could stand to benefit from learning about the pitfalls of the superficial infatuation. No matter how much the individual might think himself rooted in love, an affinity to an incomplete 'portrait' of a person is still problematic. Indeed, this dynamic is no respecter of class or status, so anyone can confuse this defective attraction with an authentic regard for the whole individual.

In order to *maintain a focus on the whole person*, one should strive to accurately perceive all attributes, place them into larger categories so as to make identification that much easier, and then to ascertain how each sex interprets these attributes. Attributes or traits are simple observations about another person, such as 'generally even-tempered, except at work', 'very sensitive about appearance, but otherwise takes criticism well', 'thrifty in all areas', 'easily swayed by opinions of other people', 'likes to read historical novels', 'very good musician but does not have discipline to develop talent.' From these observations we gain an understanding of the forces inside a person, and these forces we relate to our own drives, desires, goals, hopes, and views. All traits can be classified as facilitating, non-facilitating, promoting, or not promoting a constructive relationship between a man and woman.

Yet, because many desire to maximise their freedom, those traits that interfere with independence, even if they facilitate companionship, will be ignored or made negative. Hence, it is absolutely essential to understand how the desire for independence and the desire for love interact. Independence creates restrictions on the way in which another person is viewed. The more keenly one desires independence, the more likely it is that one will view a possible love interest only as a subset of attributes. Because of this strategy, great freedom can occur, and there is still the potential for establishing a basic relationship with the intended person. However, *as true love can come only from full respect, and as respect can come only from an evaluation of all traits, this simplified view of another person will definitely not lead to lasting, deep affection.* A full assessment of all factors must be made if one is to be happy in matrimony, and we must be assiduous in discovering those important life situations where such improper valuation of traits can arise. We fall in love with someone because we find their attributes worthy of respect, but the recognition of these attributes is affected by our desire for individuality and autonomy; thus, it is critical that we make certain our *evaluation* of another person is not affected by our particular material and emotional requirements.

Consequently, one must guard against allowing prejudices to influence judgement in this most important male-female 'enterprise'. All attributes must be considered on how they might benefit the relationship. The attraction to an attribute might be the result of it being congruent with one's own qualities, or being non-congruent. Due to the diversity of traits among people, even in the most homogenous culture, there is a low probability of making a perfect, or near-perfect, match. Therefore, if attraction between human males and females is nearly universal, then this attraction must be the result of a combination of similarity and difference. Attraction in the human realm is unique, however. We can easily observe something else in nature: Animals will invariably attempt to mate with those opposite-sex animals of like physical characteristics, keeping sexual activity within the same species or breed. No prompting other than from physiology is required for an animal to select another of its breed and to mate, which is based upon matching, through the senses various, external traits to its own. Nevertheless, animals, unlike humans, have no comprehension of 'self', and so the matching that occurs is purely mechanical. One could extrapolate this to the area of human nature, deducing that as humans have similar fundamental physiological attributes to animals (mammals), that they also have an innate proclivity to mate with their own species, and possibly their own 'breed' or race. In regards to this, we can cite a certain natural human narcissism portrayed in the arts, made obvious in the tendency for artists to render subjects in paintings with physical characteristics similar to that of the artist himself.[4] In any event, fulfilment in human relations must integrate dissimilarity, an issue that is difficult to discuss rationally because disagreement in opinions and behaviour is far more likely to cause conflict than agreement. It is this diversity, however, that puzzles and aggravates, because all too often it is that which first attracts, and then is abandoned as the couple seek similarity, either real or imagined. In essence, similarity draws a man and woman together, but it is a *constructive diversity* between them that pulls them in beyond the 'outer perimeter', and keeps them together. Similarity is easy to live with, but differences can be difficult to negotiate, yet one is eager to find those essential differences that *compensate* for weakness, thus making similitude secondary.

What has always happened through European history, continues to happen today: Men attempt to learn about women, women about men, young about old, old about young, introverted about extroverted, extroverted about introverted, and so on. Yet, these searches have taken on a new urgency, which is not surprising in an age when most people for the first 20 years or so of life seek to find out what 'me' really signifies. Eventually, they will have to learn about others for their own advantage. Although there is no shortage of works on the subject of marriage and relationships, they have for the most part failed to inform people about the real problems that exist. Ideas about independence and marriage are spread through society informally and through the mass media, so it is not as if there is no attention paid to the various factors governing the relationships between men and women. Indeed, academic works deliberate a wide variety of attributes. However, no one focusses on the concept of independence as a major source of this conflict, nor does anyone mention the often-seen negative attributes of selfishness, subjectivity, and inflexibility. Many modern writers attempt to act as clearinghouses of ideas, pandering to various groups, giving them the information that they want to hear, thus elucidating and validating self-orientated attitudes of ignorance and prejudice. Only when both authors and readers focus on a *subset* of personality traits do we get such a regrettable situation. Humanity will nonetheless always find ways and means to discuss the all-important issues of love.

Ultimately, seekers of truth need to be their own guides in formulating a viable plan which will lead them to successfully reach their goals. They must reflect on a number of issues: Is any significant adjustment in life necessary; is this adjustment possible; how long this adjustment will take; what resources will be required for the adjustment. Every person must determine what underlying principles are involved in a situation, so that specialised, even individualised, techniques of dealing with problems can be efficiently developed. One would think this varied approach is common in a society that places so much value, ironically enough, on independence of thought. Yet, people depend on others for critical answers, because they have become so 'self-governing' that they now are without knowledge of the traditional wisdom necessary for attaining genuine happiness. Accordingly, in this book we seek to explore the pertinent historical, cultural, and material aspects of the issues raised so far: The conflict between virtue and self-centeredness; the mistake of being attracted to only a few traits and not to the whole person; and most importantly, the struggle to reconcile the desire for independence, and the need for companionship and support. In order to attain a larger, more comprehensive understanding, we will at the end of our investigation distill the cross-influences affecting relationships, and put together the information that we will by then have compiled, setting it in the framework of personal development and cognisance. Consequently, the ideal of love must be carefully and objectively examined.

Chapter 2

The Ideal of Love

*I*deals are standards of excellence that act as guides to our goals in life. Reconciling these 'perfect' concepts with each other might be difficult, especially when the ideals are independence and love. Indeed, this happy joining of the desire for status and power with the desire for full companionship and cooperation today is considered inappropriate, even impossible. Notwithstanding the common thinking today that the two ideals cannot be reconciled, neither ideal can be totally rejected. Further, the truth, as perceived in historical culture, is that the efficiency and effectiveness gained in the realm of worldly affairs can maintain love and affection in the family sphere. What do we believe then, recent popular speculation, or centuries-old accumulated wisdom?

It should be obvious that the reification of an ideal (i.e. to turn something abstract into something real) is a complex endeavour, but let us make plain what is at stake. Love and independence are two universal forces, which although always in competition are not mutually incompatible. The key to accomplishing a balance of the two areas lies in discerning the nature of each. For love to exist there must be respect, and respect grows out of witnessing virtuous behaviour, such as honesty, integrity and purity. On the other hand, for personal freedom to be maximised, the individual must properly manage financial, educational, and other factors, by displaying abilities in leadership, systematic enquiry, and constructive social criticism. It is therefore critical that the individual conscientiously utilise those resources under his control. Hence, in life there will always be something of a contest between love and independence, which should be worked out into balance by compromise.

In spite of the many difficulties in matching reality and ideals, the elusive dream, to love and be loved, is not impossible to secure, however. There must be ways to make the dream come alive, as many quite obviously do, even in our fractious age. What secret methods are used to achieve the ideas begun by those fleeting glances, idle daydreams, and hopeful imaginings? What does one do when the remarkably clear vision of the future fades? In order to find out, we must show some courage and don the outfit of the explorer, for there are evidently no easily perceptible answers. The danger is that explorers are often tempted to stray, and in this case, to fall into the false belief that one can become independent of love. If there were easy answers, there is little doubt that the actual relationship between man and woman would routinely match the vision. Instead, the vision is so often and blatantly violated, that special citations and awards should be handed out to the few who reach the ideal. We must venture throughout all the areas that men and women find themselves, all the areas that affect their friendship. The aim is to find these *concealed* properties, to ascertain what establishes and rules the relationship between the sexes. Just as men and women currently have no limitations placed on them as to what they are, where they go, what they buy, what they wear, and what influences them, so this enquiry cannot have limits. It is necessary for the 'explorer' to make an examination of every important and relevant facet of another person's domain.

Thus, every person's life must be examined comprehensively, a determination of both concepts and accomplishment. It cannot be overstressed that *one person can only truly love another when both exhibit a full range of constructive ideals that match behaviour.* But difficult challenges might befall anyone, and so it is necessary to discuss each area of possible conflict, so that these can be resolved with definitude. For those who still do not understand the necessity of virtue, the dangers of relying solely on material factors must be shown to them. For those who do understand virtue, their comprehension should be reinforced, in order to preempt the problems that could arise in those areas that are still weak.

The matters that enter into *properly founded* relationships can challenge individual lives, but should not and cannot undermine the love and affection that exist, as long as there is adherence to the seven virtues, a prerequisite for all authentic intimate relationships. 'Pure love' is undefiled dearness, or being cherished with an emotion unadulterated by social obligation; material and pragmatic factors, such as status, are never more important than the love itself. Such love is beyond mere attraction, and moves into the deepest realm of human existence. It is our goal to see that men and woman can attain this through their own efforts, while still remaining cognisant of their own needs, and operating within the boundaries of traditional morality. Thus, the intent of any discussions on relationships should be to provide the means to achieve *authentic* intimacy and affection, which is indeed the greatest achievement of mankind.

Yet, certain factors, often related to social pressure, interfere with choice, and also might make living a virtuous life difficult. Compromises are often made to moral principles, in order to support the vitality of the machine-driven industrial economy. People can foolishly give up their own minds and bodies in return for what they consider to be satisfaction. The individual can be swayed in many directions, but it should always be kept in mind that people exercise Free Will in regard to their decisions, this idea always being present in the history of Western civilisation. Free Will is tied to autonomy; when one has no binding ties, one is then theoretically free to make choices amongst viable alternatives.

The concepts of 'love' or 'companionship' do not demand a socially determined formal arrangement; nonetheless, the relationship may become 'official' at some point. Yet, people cannot be limited by weaknesses in modalities. Even though we use terms relating to married life as indicative of the close relationship between a man and woman, such a relationship can take place in *any* social circumstance. Western society, or Anglophone society at any rate, does not have any other convenient expression for 'a close bond between a man and woman', beyond that of calling the persons involved a 'husband', 'wife', or 'spouse'. As a result, when we say the tendency to 'marry', this, in reality, means the tendency to become emotionally and intellectually devoted to another, whether formally married, only cohabiting, or in some other arrangement.

Thus, although love is predicated on feeling, it must begin with a very tangible interconnection, and a variety of issues in reference to the other person must be evaluated before intimacy can occur. Undoubtedly, *the pursuit of marriage entails a rational process which requires objectivity and, just as importantly, flexible and innovative use of resources*. Yet, substantial social pressures can alter this search process, inducing intimacy-averse persons into marriage. European society has long offered a succession of life path opportunities in order to give the individual the chance to reach the optimum, in both emotional and materialistic matters. Therefore, the interrelationship of economics and culture, in such areas as occupation, income, savings, and mortality, has exerted only a moderate effect on marriage patterns (see Sporer 2010A).

In modern society, however, success based on skill and merit may be elusive, and external factors, not choice, often affect career and social pathways. These issues begin early and one's experiences in the family home will considerably impact one's attitudes to married life and society in general. Even a person's first sign of independence, that of leaving the home of origin to begin a new living situation, is an event often influenced by social pressure to contribute to the economy, but also by feelings of dissatisfaction with home life. Nonetheless, an emotionally inadequate upbringing may increase the desire for a companionate relationship, as a means of providing the love one never received at home.

Hence, marriage decisions are often not rationally based, i.e., they are affected by factors that are unrelated to a future spouse, and the dynamic of achieving wholeness, through the joining of appropriate traits, is often ignored. As a result, various neglected psychological and personality issues must be investigated in order to understand how to bring reason back into the process. We can say that alterations in society and economy have succeeded in creating an emphasis on attitudes which assure larger group solidarity, and not marital harmony. Concepts of autonomy have been bolstered, which in the modern context produces exploitation of the kindness of others, and a derogation of constructive inter-dependence. Two critical personality issues, personal sacrifice and the willingness to change, have been abandoned. Because of these negative actions, it is now believed that, although friendships of all kinds are important, marriage is the only relationship where the ideal of love can be satisfied, as other types of relations have become more unstable and distant (see Sporer 2010A, 2010B). Unfortunately, the selfishness which operates so freely in this world cannot be contained to life outside the home, and overbearing self-interest can weaken and degrade the husband-wife relationship.

However, these developments should not prevent us from objectively assessing all the aspects of 'independence' and 'dependence'. Independence means to do the things, to possess the things, and surround oneself with the people, that one desires. Dependence means to rely on the emotional, intellectual, and material support of another, including advice, validation of ideas, direction, inspiration, and financial support. The ideal of love, which is that most profound desire to have an intimate and fulfilling relationship with someone, must not to be overwhelmed by the desire for independence, as it must not fall into abject dependence. Throughout time, independence, dependence, and love have co-existed, and this will continue to be true as long as there are human beings. In the past, people were able to pursue an independent livelihood, a position of respectability in society, and substantive support from others, while simultaneously maintaining a loving, unique relationship with a husband or wife.

In our day the theme of independence has become a preoccupation, which in turn has made it difficult to be loved because there is a lack of trust and respect. People have made themselves 'unlovable' because of the deceit, frivolity, aloofness, self-centeredness, and promiscuity that society expects of the fully 'autonomous' person. True love in this case is impossible, and instead a negative form of dependence is used as a substitute. A couple's activities *might* be undertaken with cooperation and convergence of interests in mind, but more likely, in the modern age, they are carried out on the principle of a *quid pro quo*, where the two take turns satisfying each other's self-centred needs. Interestingly, although both sexes have undergone significant changes in personal ideals, it is women who have experienced the greater transformation, discarding idealism in favour of pragmatism.

We can conclude that a detailed strategy—containing principles, approaches, tactics, alternatives, defences—that leads to the balancing and reconciling of the great ideals of life must be devised. Therefore, careful attention must be paid to the hazards society emplaces on one segment of the journey of life, that long stretch of road that leads to the joining of independence and love. This road, however, unlike many others, can be travelled quite within the capacity of the average individual, and it is not particularly arduous; there are traps of course along the route, although not that many in number. The turns and twists are easily comprehensible because they are so basic to individual life: Education, leaving the family home, establishing friendships, building a career, saving money, improving quality of life, etc. Sovereignty over one's affairs is indeed possible, not because one merely *knows* about these issues, but because one *authoritatively controls the consequences of the issues* through the use of intellect.

Contemplating these social influences is highly important, yet we should not take anything for granted. Assistance from other sources should always be welcome. The advantageous aspect about the sociological study is that everyone can bring something of his or her own to it. Indeed, one of the best ways to determine whether a theory is correct is simply to see if it can be applied to one's own life. This is what sets the social sciences apart from all other disciplines, which demand controlled scientific examination for verification. However, experts can only attempt to realistically set the *context* wherein resolution of challenges to one's concepts of affection and autonomy can fruitfully occur, but the individual is responsible for correct application of the principles found by others.

Hence, unless one understands all the substantive factors involved in the relationship between men and women *in reference to one's own personal needs*, one will undoubtedly risk great failure. This is not a selfish attitude. We should always bear in mind, that although love never requires justification, each turn we take on the road of life must be defensible. Yet how can we make correct decisions without knowing our own interests, strengths, and weaknesses? If one comprehends the truth, and it is not an onerous task, one stands an excellent chance of protecting oneself from emotional and material injury, and finally achieving one's ideal of love.

We have seen in this chapter that *reason* and *objectivity* must govern the pursuit that seeks to balance the factors of life into harmonious relationship. Such logic necessitates following a *clear sequence of events*, with a steady focus on objective; approaches characterised by carelessness and indifference should be rejected. The first step we take is to recognise the unalterable conditions of that govern all close relationships. Let us now explore the various aspects of relationship construction as found in European traditions, a subject which is surprisingly misunderstood.

Chapter 3

Friendship and Courtship

*S*everal principles that affect the formation of relationships here need to be elucidated. Firstly, people desire affection in whatever form it comes, and from whatever source. Children, insecure and defenceless, will seek the affection of parents and relatives, hoping to receive the protection they desire. Secondly, if the attention is adequate and instrumental, then these children will be less likely to seek affection outside the home. Thirdly, as they grow older, they gradually become more interested in gaining independence, but if home life is attractive, there is little reason why they should seek out friends from the social environment, unless they come up to the standard to which they are accustomed.

The background to all this, however, must contain the freedom to choose and explore relationships between children, parents, relatives, and friends. This type of 'liberty' in home life becomes a critical component in the development of healthy concepts of love and affection. Consequently, the general parameters of relationships are established early in life, and are in many ways based on experiences in the household of childhood.

Although home life is influential, many of the requirements that the individual wants to satisfy in a relationship are derived from intensely personal desires. Males and females often come together because they find that the similitude in thoughts and feelings cross-validate individual desires. The ideas of one person are echoed by the other; the seemingly impermeable wall that prevents under-

standing can be demolished by the knowledge of the other; observations can be taken and completed, and given insight by the other.
The liaison between a man and woman can therefore be extremely
consequential. As Lucretius rightly observed: *Consuetudo concinnat
amorem*, that is, *habit causes love*. One is intuitively drawn into
deepening the relationship for these reasons, magnifying and expanding the positive experiences one has had. At some point there
must be a resolution to the question: Are we to go forward into
intimacy, or are we to remain merely acquaintances? If substantial
resources are expended on behalf of the other person, usually the
inclination is to proceed and open oneself up emotionally, materially, and physically. Thus, all *intimate relationships*, including
marriage arranged freely, must begin with *friendship*.

Logic would seem to indicate that love falls on a continuum of
relationship closeness. Before we can convince ourselves that love
is truly an integral part of the relationship, a considerable investment of resources must be made, although according to La Bruyère
we would be wasting our time: 'Love begins with love; friendship,
however warm, cannot change to love, however mild.' This overly
idealistic attitude towards love posits that compatibility is *instantly*
recognisable, so one knows immediately if a relationship is bound
for love or for mere friendship. But to believe this would indeed be
folly, for as we have said, it is absolutely essential that we found
our affections on the basis of evaluating *all of a person's traits*, and
it is impossible to know these traits before numerous meetings and
discussions have taken place. No one, unless he is a suspect in a
criminal case, is compelled to reveal details of his life, and such
revelations usually must come under the aegis of friendship. Consequently, since friendship is not compulsory, whilst the evaluation
process is going on, there are two basic principles that are active
and determine whether our investment is prudent, and whether the
friendship bond will be deepened into love: The *degree of commitment* one can expect from the other person in pursuing and main-

taining the relationship, and the *risk of losing* that person's friendship to another. These issues, of commitment and stability, are
made reasonable, because they stem from a fundamental knowledge of human nature, and relationships cannot go further without
them being resolved. It is rather evident that they form the over-
arching themes for every companionate relationship, being present
whether acknowledged or not. Within a dyad (two-person relationship), there are four possible issues:

Table 1. Factors involved in deepening a friendship:
　　　　Entrustment and concentration of attention

	Degree of commitment of the other person to this relationship	Probability of the other person forming another relationship
Man	A (high/low)	B (high/low)
Woman	C (high/low)	D (high/low)

The cells contain the following definitions:
A. Man's expectation of a woman's commitment to him
B. Man's expectation of a woman going to another man
C. Woman's expectation of a man's commitment to her
D. Woman's expectation of a man going to another woman

The *best* relationship would be one where both the man and the
woman feel that the other is highly committed to the relationship,
and is at low risk of becoming involved with someone else (eg high
A, low B). The worst relationship would be one where both the
man and woman feel that the other is poorly committed to the
relationship, and is at high risk to become involved with someone
else (eg low C, high D).

Commitment, or more accurately entrustment, is a pledge to take a certain course of action in the future, with implied penalties if one does not. Male-female relationships demand a larger set of promises than other relationships; they must abide by certain rules concerning the amount of time, support, praise, consideration, advice and money one person gives to another. In regard to the other factor, the loss of someone involves a complete, or nearly complete, abandonment. There might be some future contact, but intimacy is limited, and information and opinions are restricted.

The two factors of commitment and risk of loss are largely independent. Let us examine a few unexpected combinations. One could be poorly committed to a relationship, yet not be very prone to start a committed (exclusive) relationship with another person (low commitment, low risk of loss). This scenario is more likely to occur when independence is an important goal in life. When independence is high, then there is a tug of war between two factors: The individual and another person, or the individual and a situation, such as a career. For example, if a woman is dividing her attention between two men, $A <- F -> B$, and she wishes to obtain satisfaction from A, but also likes to do the same with B, then there can be little or no commitment to either, lest they bog her down. It should be understood, however, that she might not wish to leave either man, so her chance of ending a relationship is low, although her level of commitment is also low. Further, one could be highly committed to someone and still be attracted to another person (high commitment, high risk of loss), a state of affairs which occurs when there is a sense of duty, but inadequate knowledge about, and valuation of, the first relationship. Thus, self-centeredness is the source of the problem in the first situation, and ignorance is the source of the problem in the second.

Once a friendship is established, and the individual feels that there is a future for the couple, the themes of entrustment and fidelity become even more significant as the level of investment increases. *The level of continued entrustment is often predicated on how easily an individual can find another person that will be at least an equal substitute.* Based on utilitarian concepts, if the male presence is low, and female presence high, then it is easy for any particular man to find another woman, accordingly making his commitment to his current female partner fairly low. When companionship is valued highly and people become 'cost-conscious', each individual assigns a certain approximate probability to finding another friend of the opposite sex if the present one is lost. For example, there is a 20% chance of a woman losing a man due to a small surplus of females in the community; a woman with a very high educational attainment will have reason to worry, for she knows the difficulty that awaits in finding another available man with similar educational status, if the current relationship misfires. She could well engage in physical intimacy in order to deepen the bond and increase the man's commitment (a situation which creates a form of pseudo-marriage). On the other hand, a woman of average education might not turn to such a manipulative enterprise in order to 'capture' a man, because if her boyfriend leaves her, the loss would not be onerous. The cost of finding another man of *average* education (as opposed to *high* education) is low, as there are greater numbers of such men, compared to the numbers of men of *low* or *high* educational attainment.

Thus, we can say that there are two types of cross-sex relationship: Friend and lover. The divergent responsibilities of each leaves a clear social dichotomy, that only the most foolhardy persons would dare to ignore. Although it is common for single men and women to go out frequently on dates, any longer-term dating relationship necessitates reflections on marriage. There must be flexibility, a *change* from friendship to 'lover-ship'. Unfortunately, in an independence-driven society where the numbers of males and females are generally the same, the attempt to 'deepen' a relationship usually results in a vacillation in attitudes and behaviour, with commitment flickering like a flame. Consequently, for the sake of harmony, a discerning and sympathetic relationship should proceed with the understanding that both partners are readying for life-long entrustment. The friendly form of the relationship requires a *resolution* to enquiries and challenges, but not necessarily commitment.

The pathway of 'lover-ship' is known as courting, a period of time during which the couple get to know one another, their backgrounds, their likes and dislikes, their attitudes, their hopes and fears. It is a series of informal meetings between members of the opposite sex that fundamentally are a loosening, if not a rejection, of the individual's independence, and are usually a prelude to more intimate relations and marriage. If the couple feel that they are then able to live with each other, and if they feel that they cannot live without each other (a 'romantic' notion), and if the fundamental pragmatic factors are in place (e.g. the availability of housing, jobs, income for food and clothing, furniture), then they would consent to marry.

The context and timing in which the 'dating' occurs are often socially and culturally determined. There is great variation of form, ranging from meetings planned and supervised closely by parents, to fully independent decision-making by young people. In times past, men and women met in informal situations at people's homes, at gatherings, and in church. There were no clubs, bars, dating services or other means, and connections were usually arranged by family members. Such contact through personal networks meant that the door of one's home could admit many potential partners and suitors in safety and discretion. In European cultures, the tradition has been one that stressed close guardianship, but it has never included or tolerated actual decision-making by parents as a general rule. Unless a society was on the verge of penury, or relatively great fortunes were involved, people saw fit to allow their children to marry whom they wished, although the voicing of an opinion about the relationship was not uncommon.

However, dating forms only one aspect of courtship. Courtship can be seen as a process encompassing a number of factors: Understanding each other, increasing desire for each other's company, establishing the rules of the relationship, and preparing the way for marriage and lifetime companionship. Flexibility in the form of *mental adjustments* must always precede material changes, and so time must be given for rearrangement of internal and external resources and dynamics. Independence is an asset in this case, as it allows an individual the time to complete the stages of courtship, and to walk away from the relationship if serious problems come to be revealed. This process can be broken down into the following phases: *Exploration, Assessment, Building, Execution* (the use of the masculine pronoun below is for convenience; of course, the same points apply to women as well).

A. EXPLORATION. To *find* another person that meets the minimum criteria of 'goodness' for a mate.

The individual searches for a person that will meet his standards, which might include level of extroversion, ambition, career plans, material philosophy, views on children, home life, social life, politics, morals and ethics. He can use a variety of resources, such as friends' recommendations, personal statements, or biographies. Although it can last several years, this phase is probably the most important since a high achievement here will mean much lower level of effort in later phases. There is no a priori time limit, apart from the one culture might impose, because there is no control over the variety of people one is likely to encounter. Much is based on probability, although one can increase the odds of finding individuals who meet the requirements by engaging third parties in the search. Care must be taken to verify all pertinent characteristics; untruthfulness and inaccuracy, things one must always guard against, can be very common in self-descriptions.

B. ASSESSMENT. To *discover* what the individual will find necessary to adjust in his life, in order to have a successful marriage.

Needless to say, no one will ever perfectly fit one's criteria. No
matter how well one explores, one will frequently have to make
certain sacrifices to accommodate the essential hopes of the other
person. Thus, the individual must now understand what he will
have to do to please the other person. This could mean changes in
school plans, career goals, leisure time, time spent socialising; it
might mean delaying certain activities he now takes for granted.
If he is able to accept these changes then he can move on to the
next phase, if not then the courtship should be ended. This phase
can last a few months. Since the particulars of his potential mate
have been verified in the previous phase, the individual, who presumably knows himself better than he knows anyone else, can
fairly quickly resolve what changes must be made and whether he
can or cannot tolerate them.

C. BUILDING. To *prepare* to implement the necessary changes
in lifestyle and personality.

The individual must now make allowances in his behaviour and
possibly find alternatives to his original life goals. If his future wife
insists on him getting a better education, for example, he will have
to look for a school and the funding. If she wishes for him to stop
spending so much time with his friends, he will have to ease himself out of these relationships without giving offense. He will have
to prepare himself psychologically for a new life. The temporal
extent of this phase is the most unpredictable. Depending on what
changes were agreed upon, it might last from a few weeks to many
years. In previous generations, couples would remain engaged for
years, until they felt that they had obtained a requisite amount of
academic education, secured good employment, and had saved
enough money to buy or rent a residence that was to their liking.

D. EXECUTION. To *implement* the changes in lifestyle that a person has agreed to make.

If both people have made earnest attempts at change, if they have fully cooperated, there is an excellent chance that the marriage will be successful; more successful, in fact, than either could have imagined. This phase should clearly begin before marriage, although realistically it will probably be several years before all the changes have finally been made. It is not uncommon that in the first three to five years of married life, both husband and wife tend to maintain a significant variability in traits, after which they tend to converge more.[5] *A* wishes *B* to change his behaviour, which *B* does, thus pleasing *A*; this works for awhile, but then *B* finds it difficult, so reverts back to old ways or turns to some other unacceptable manner of behaviour. *B* tries again to change, but this time with a different approach, which succeeds in the longer term.

Hence, beginning with a cursory examination of another person, one moves to simple friendship, on to deeper friendship, and then finally to marriage. In all phases there must be the consideration of how likely it is that this friend will leave for another, and how seriously this person takes the nature of the relationship. Further, the pace of the phases is predicated to a certain extent on one or the other finding alternative partners; this probability might actually increase with growing friendship, as one can look for someone new as weaknesses are revealed.

Let us now look at a real life example showing the operation of these factors, as few studies have investigated modern courtship practises in tradition based cultures. Where studies have been made, their focus on the courtship situation is restricted to material considerations, thus ignoring emotional and psychological changes.

A community in Andalusia[6] is probably representative of a modern culture grounded in traditional mores mirroring a pre-modern rural society, especially one which accepted marriage later in life.

People in this region have conservative social values, separate roles according to sex, but young people still easily fraternise with one another, limiting social intercourse after courtship begins. They show great care in choosing a mate, going through a lengthy courtship process that might easily last five to seven years. Research has identified three stages in courtship: The secret phase, lasting six months to a year, where a man and woman meet informally, usually without the knowledge or explicit approval of parents (corresponding to phase A above); the romantic phase, lasting one to two years, where the formal courtship begins (as a lead-in to marriage) and the couple intensify their relationship, become comfortable with each other's personalities and temperaments, and where the families get to know one another (B and C above); the contribution phase, lasting one to four years, where arrangements are made procuring the house, furniture, and so on (D above). During this last phase, the economic status of each family is assessed, and the families then come to some kind of an agreement as to what each will contribute, with an emphasis on complete fairness. The woman and her family are often expected to supply furnishings, and the man and his family are expected to provide the residence. Preparation usually begins even before the couple begin their courtship, but intensifies once the couple decide to eventually marry.[7]

The social focus is on phases C and D, and courtship is an informal, but by no means casual, contract, where each party is expected to provide certain minimum contributions as set by culture, and other contributions as promised. It is apparent that people are not especially fearful of losing a potential mate to someone else, nor do people seem to lack commitment. Starting the marriage out well in the material domain is uppermost in everyone's mind, and indeed, the problems of adjustment that occur in the first years of marriage can be magnified if the couple struggles to find acceptable living quarters, buy furniture and other items, or to live up to a desired standard. In this particular culture, inheritance is a trou-

bling issue, the root of many family problems, with siblings quarrel-
ling over shares. Community members are careful to be quiet about
their household affairs as envy is rampant; even the realisation of
small differences between households can precipitate acrimonious
relations. These observations might very well be true in many other
regions, but to a certain extent reflect the temperament, and so the
innate character of the people.

Hence, it would at least appear that *exogenous* variables have a
major influence on the courtship process, that the economy and
culture are tangible factors when it comes to the courtship process.
Naturally, the psychological needs of the individual are paramount,
but many other factors could affect the desire to marry, other than
to maintain a deep friendship with the opposite sex. We can imag-
ine, however, that the specific primary needs for companionship
can be buried under other considerations, which can ultimately
wreak havoc with those primary needs. Consequently, one must
examine many of the significant factors that are external to the
specific decision to maintain this intimate and enduring relationship. *Nonetheless, basic psychological principles of evaluating entrustment and fidelity, as discussed above, are always active.*

To fully comprehend the processes of courtship, the main regula-
tors of the phenomenon must be sought. Economic and cultural
factors are mainly responsible for the length of courtship, and the
rules of courtship can be affected. Indeed, courtship *length* is a
common factor affecting many aspects of this process, including
level of emotional intimacy, finances, family relations, and organi-
sation of life plans. In this case, people must abide by the demands
of material necessity as to how long it will take to reach the personal ideal. The better the economy, the shorter the courtship
period, other things being the same. Psychological factors are often
not openly addressed, with the old assumption being made that the
couple will 'grow' in love. When the process is longer, greater
attention can then be given to developing understanding of the

other's personality and needs, greater closeness can be achieved, and greater augmentation of material resources is possible.

Thus, the level of social interaction also governs the courtship. If a particular social situation requires waiting a long period, then the sexes must be rather aloof; if they were not, early infatuation and love interest could spark early marriage (if premarital sex is strongly condemned). Where the ideal *material* life can be reached quickly (standards are low, and/or the economy is doing extremely well), then division between the sexes is not mandatory. However, in a culture which demands *compatibility,* it would appear that separation of the sexes is necessary so that matching of traits can be ascertained; such limitations usually do not preclude ordinary friendship. Further, this same separation encourages and facilitates independence, since one is presumably freed from early marriage.

From a circle of friends, a man and woman choose and accept each other as marriage partners. He and she both work and save to put together a home that is consistent with their goals of comfort and aesthetics; when they accumulate what is required, they then marry and move into their new residence. A plausible sequence seems to obtain: Standard of living concepts force young people to wait a while before marrying, and the culture pressures men and women to remain apart, somewhat distant from one another. The sequence might be as follows:

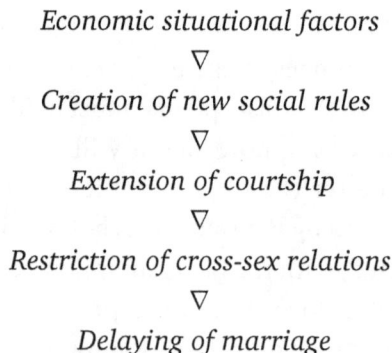

Economic situational factors

∇

Creation of new social rules

∇

Extension of courtship

∇

Restriction of cross-sex relations

∇

Delaying of marriage

Although the economy has some role to play in how people socialise (e.g. there is a positive correlation between number of close friends and GNP per capita), the argument that work and money are highly significant factors regulating contact between the sexes is evidently false (see Sporer 1999).

We have seen that the length and rules of courtship are thought to be influenced by the degree to which the sexes fraternise. The issue might be one of simple availability: the more friends one has, the earlier one's marriage. However, if the intention is to hasten marriage by allowing access between the sexes, then it does not work in certain places, such as Andalusia. Possibly they are by nature more restrained, thus holding back on forming intimate relations. They might also be culturally more predisposed to take care in going through the phases of courtship, without pressure.

Research shows that among the larger Western nations, when a person has relatively *few* male and female friends, it is *less likely* that he or she will marry late.[8] In other words, *people who have few friends are likely to marry earlier, and people who have many friends often delay marriage.* The stronger the correlation of marriage with a measured external variable (number of friends), the likelier it appears that some segment of a population is strongly affected by one variable, and that one alone. This is not to say that there is not some other segment of the population where having more friends will lead to earlier marriage (there is no clear correlation for marrying at ages below 30), but we can conclude that there is at least one segment that will see friendship as a substitute for marriage. Nonetheless, certain internal influences, not easily measured, might also have a role. It is quite possible that the external parameters of a friendship circle are largely affected by personal choice. In this regard, we need to examine more closely other factors in addition to size and depth of friendship interaction. Indeed, personality might determine the strength of desire for opposite-sex friendship, which in turn affects marriage age.

The act of choosing one's friends is one probably of the freest things that one can do, not affected by economic considerations, living conditions, and so on, then the possibility arises that friend choice is the result of *temperament,* i.e. genetically influenced. In addition, if a strong correlation between friendship choice and marriage exists, other factors are of little or no influence; with no other forces that would work to affect the choice of friends (and so indirectly marriage age), the idea that this choice is the product of some individual innate dynamic is strengthened. Hence, it is probable that the 'aloofness' in relations between the sexes, and indeed the courtship process as a whole, that exists in certain countries, might be the product of innate genetic traits, and it is the individual's personality then that 'calls the shots'. The rules of courtship are both a cause and effect in many matters in a young person's life, but in light of these observations about personality, it would now appear that they are more an effect than a cause.

Even if there are rigid rules of manners and etiquette that draw boundaries on physical intimacy, this does not mean that men and women cannot have close emotional relationships which adequately fulfill their *innate or temperamental desires* so that marriage is made unnecessary. Consequently, friendship can act, not only as a way to attract a potential mate and to bring about courtship, but it can also serve as a *substitute* for marriage itself. During courtship, however, the couple might isolate themselves from their friends, focussing their attention on one another. The true sequence of events delaying marriage might be described as follows:

Temperamental factors

∇

Adjustments on circle of friends

∇

Lengthening of courtship or delaying of marriage

As for the last point above, we can say that if cross-sex relations are limited in scope by personal disposition and/or social rules, and courtship is the only legitimate context in which a close friendship can take place between young men and women, then courtship would likely be extended, and the saving of money is simply the best use of this time, but not an end in itself. Further, restraints placed on meetings between long-affianced couples might be a prudent measure to reduce the temptation to engage in sexual intimacy before marriage. Thus, separation might be more necessary between engaged people, than between opposite-sex friends.

Let us now examine the most visible element of 'temperament' or 'personal disposition', that of *extroversion*. Intuitively, we might say that those who are introverted will often have fewer opposite sex friends, and therefore will not marry early. But is this really the case? An introverted individual will prefer the company of people he knows; since other persons of the same sex will be more likely to share his beliefs and attitudes, he will more likely fraternise with them, than with the opposite sex. The introvert has fewer friends than the extrovert, which leads him to seek marriage, but his *personality* prevents facilitation of this. When he finally does find an opposite-sex close friend, he is more likely to formalise the relationship by initiating courtship, and this often leads to marriage, since he would not wish to lose this close friend.

One could then think that having a greater number of opposite sex friends would *increase* the likelihood of early marriage, with an extrovert having more potential partners from which to choose, compared to an introvert. This assessment would be logical if based on a materialistic analysis, but further research reveals that this does not seem to be the case. Extroversion is strongly related to having a larger number of close friends, but is only modestly associated with early marriage.[9] As mentioned above, the individual can focus on the ability of friendship to act as a substitute for marriage, and indeed this process seems more likely for extroverts.

Thus, the personality trait of extroversion deals with freedom of personal relations and the width of a friendship circle. The extrovert might call upon a number of opposite sex friends for advice, comfort, and so on, not necessarily imposing himself on any one friend that much. An introvert might obtain all of his friendship from one other person; such a relationship would entail a formalisation because of the sacrifice involved. When the level of closeness and sacrifice demanded by another person crosses a threshold, the relationship then moves from friendship to love interest, and to maintain the relation, courtship must begin. Yet, courtship and marriage narrow the friendship circle, regardless of whether one or both people are introverted.[10] Consequently, the size of the friendship circle affects marriage, but marriage also affects the size of the friendship circle. We can see a close connection between companionate relations and social environment.

The extrovert's tendency to speak openly and freely widens the circle of friends, making reliance on any one friend unnecessary. The same tendency, however, allows the extrovert to become very close with one or two people in this circle, especially with the opposite sex, necessitating a *reduction* in the size of his circle. Naturally, the extrovert could find great satisfaction in just one very close friendship, but he also prefers having many other friendships, admittedly shallow, but nevertheless rewarding to some extent. The natural outgoingness of the extrovert makes him construct varied friendships, but his eye will fall on one friend who recommends he forsake the others, so he can spend more time with her. Therefore, he experiences a widening of the circle, then a narrowing of it, and then possibly again another widening, if this close friendship ends. We can formulate a general principle which represents the inherently mutually exclusive nature of this phenomenon. Succinctly put, it is in the extrovert's nature to desire and have many friends, but it is this wide circle and ingratiating personality that quickly allow him to gain the confidence of a *single companion, who then demands more exclusive use of this time*. After awhile, the extrovert is tempted to go back to the larger circle of friends, as per his usual nature. If excessive independence (and by extension inflexibility) is linked to excessive extroversion, as it often is in modern society, then this principle describes, in rough outline, the current struggle in relationships, and the harmful tension that can result between the outside world and the couple.

We can see that three factors—extroversion, size of friendship circle, and independence—are critical in defining the parameters of friendships, and in turn affecting the process of courtship. Cultural and economic aspects impact courtship, and when mixed with strong personal motivations, produce ramifications and complexities that the individual must learn to negotiate, sometimes on his own. These various factors must be consciously and objectively balanced using a combination of reason and flexibility; once again we note that the ideal companionate relationship cannot be attained through a lazy contemplation that incorporates notions, whims, and fancies into a 'strategy'.

Let us now go from 'theory' to 'practise', and examine the various real life methods that people use to attempt to build the ideal relationship, where they handle the erratic turns of personality, friendship choices, and the desire for independence, whilst manoeuvring through the 'pathway' of the four phases discussed above. We shall see that people rely on one or more of several methods: Independent assessment using reason and logic; utilisation of relevant advice, support, and assistance; tacit acceptance of the unpredictable events of chance, luck, or fate. Of course, even when the most sincere attempt is made to find an appropriate partner, failure is always possible, and in certain contexts, it is common. As a result, we shall also discuss the psychological areas that are impacted by the inability to reach one's ideal of intimacy, that is, when the desire to liberate love from the confines of social roles and materialism is thwarted.

Chapter 4

Building an Intimate Relationship

*T*hrough the process of courtship, an individual's level of entrustment and extent of attention are discovered; the courtship itself is taken at a pace decided largely by the individual himself, in accordance with his level of extroversion. Hence, *the role of materialism is often secondary to the functions of emotions and personality.* Attention should, therefore, be paid to the mental factors, as enumerated in the four phases above (page 27), that figure into adjustment during courtship as much as the economic factors. The process will not function correctly unless and until both people substantially cooperate with each other, and as with anything else there can be no great return where there has not been significant investment. Of course, one can always be fortunate, and find a mate that has near total compatibility. But in most cases there must be give and take, without which each person will increasingly irritate and disappoint the other, leading to disagreements and animosity. Further, this procedure will often not work, when one or both have a psychological disorder. Particularly troublesome are various personality disorders which make people unstable, impulsive, defiant, weak or indecisive. Whereas many might emphasise the joys of intimate relationships, it is the role of the unbiassed researcher to bring attention to the costs as well as benefits.

How easily the individual gets along with other people, and the depth and number of friendships he has, are indicative of the dexterity and skill with which he forms relationships. The proficiency of relationship management is an important consideration determining the extent to which one methodically follows a long-term plan. If relationships are formed only with difficulty, then people will be loathe to expend large resources on analysis, as the results will often signal rejection of one person, and the search starts for yet another. It is easier, if not wiser, to eschew any complicated search process, and take whatever contact seems good. Realistically, the process which men and women utilise to make meaningful social contact with others similar to themselves is a critical factor in the long-term stability of the intimate relationship.

We have seen how phases C and D often require personal adjustments, and one might very well expect that the first two phases of courtship demand similar flexibility. Indeed, the methods used to find a spouse can be as varied as the human imagination can allow. As a way of overcoming the problems presented by shyness and poor access to the opposite sex, and as a kind of antipode to the rational search process, certain cultures stress certain alternatives to extended courtship, such as mystical procedures that 'reveal' the inevitable truth about potential matrimonial candidates, and so obviate the problems of choice. It is thought that, because of the high ideals many have about love, any error in judgement, no matter how seemingly trivial, might be fatal. As Proust said, 'It is a mistake to speak of a bad choice in love, since, as soon as a choice exists, it can only be bad.' A woman might resort to 'magic' in order to uncover the name of the man 'fated' to be her lover, or to reveal to the unwitting male the 'truth' about their inevitable future together. Thus, the belief that choice of marriage partner is *destiny* and not really in the hands of mere mortals. Psychics, numerology, astrology, and other parapsychological fields have commonly been used for many generations as both the means to secure a mate and as a means to sustain true love. People, particularly women, living in rustic cultures have been using such methods for many generations. We find that where this indirect approach to finding true love flourishes, men are more likely to obtain a mate through aggressive tactics.[11] However, since coercion is more likely to be used between people who know each other,[12] we can say that restrictive rules of courtship might not be at fault for this retreat into the primitive, since close relations are not likely to have begun at the time these weaknesses appear. Coercion of one kind or another is often used by impatient and socially unskilled individuals to get what they want, when negotiations turn out to be fruitless.

One could say that aggression is a type of 'personal adjustment' in relation to the courtship process, but this behaviour is of limited value. Aggressive tactics are more likely to be used when satisfactory contact is present between the sexes, but obtaining commitment becomes difficult, because of the demands of the social environment. Consequently, lacking physical prowess, women in unsophisticated societies manipulate preternatural and 'unseen forces' as a way of controlling men, a mysticism which men evidently accept, but which they counter with physical domination in everyday life. A cycle arises in which men fear the 'occult power' women have over them, which in turn spurs more aggression, which in turn makes women even more likely to rely on potions, spells, and so on. No doubt the infatuation that sometimes seizes men when meeting a woman appears 'irrational', and so contributes to the feeling that unnatural forces are at work.

Notwithstanding the curiously intriguing qualities of such 'moonstruck' relationships, it is much more instructive to see how a *rational plan operates*, especially one that artfully combines psychological factors with pragmatic ones, as seen in European cultures.

W. A. Mozart, the great composer, lodged for some period of time with Weber family whose household situation deteriorated after the father died. With the approval of the mother, he developed a friendship with one of the daughters. Mozart came to know the manners and personalities of the people involved: The oldest sister was insincere and something of a flirt, the youngest sister was rather unintelligent, but the middle one, Constance, was competent enough to run the whole household, yet received no recognition or reward. He believed her to be a virtuous woman, with common sense, facility with domestic crafts, and above all a sense of honour. Much of her maturity and proficiency he attributed to her having to compensate for the indolence of the others.[13] Like many others of his time, Mozart believed that difficult challenges, and with it hard work, build character. Constance's honesty appears to a natural disposition, which led her to achieve other skills out of necessity. A proposal of marriage was made by Mozart not only for his own sake, but in order to 'save her' from two bickering sisters and an overbearing mother. For a young girl, losing a father, and living with a mother and two other siblings without much financial support, would surely have created a certain loneliness. No doubt it was natural for her to make a close friendship with a respectable, artistically talented boarder.

Thus, Mozart was able to temper his idealism with practicality and good sense. He developed his friendship with Constance within the domestic situation, as was very common at that time. His career took him to many cities, which allowed him the opportunity to meet eligible women and converse with them at length, but without any obligation on his part, although occasionally his gregarious nature led some women to think he was serious in marrying them. He made a point of looking for virtuous women, those who met his traditional, religion-inspired standards. This virtuous woman would find her reward in a devoted husband who did his best to balance his ambitious career with his domestic life. Upon his marriage, Mozart transitioned smoothly into his new domestic condition, evidently not intending to make major adjustments to his habits in order to conform with his wife's requests, except perhaps acceding to her wish that he travel less frequently. We do not know if Constance insisted on any other significant changes in his behaviour, but there is little doubt that the similar backgrounds of Wolfgang

and Constance helped reduce the number of extraordinary demands in their married life. How would things have turned out had
they been of very different classes, or one highly educated and the
other not, or one English-speaking the other German-speaking? We
surmise that building the relationship would have been more difficult, but the result would have been the same.

After reviewing the evidence, we see that in any intimate relationship the key to long-term success is to first objectively determine if there is enough compatibility between the partners, and if
there is enough *flexibility* on both sides. The loss of independence
must be made up by meaningful social relations within married
life; in essence, the freedom one gives up is compensated by cooperation from a spouse, who does not constrain, but *reinforces*. Yet,
this quality is not equally perceived by both sexes. In a study of
how pressures in courtship affects life after marriage, Orbuch et al
(1993) used satisfaction in the third year of married life as a guide
to whether a match was successful. It was found that if men *initiate*
courtship and/or propose marriage, there is a *higher* chance the
relationship will succeed than if the woman does so.

Hence, it would appear that men are often more *objective* in mate
selection than women. Women might operate under more unrealistic assumptions and force a match, whereas men might be more
cognisant of the probability of a good marital relationship. It might
also be true that women show more flexibility in accommodating
themselves to a husband's personality. Mate selection is always a
two-way process; a man might be well-satisfied with a woman's
looks, background, education and temperament, but the woman
might not be content with his attributes, and she might choose
someone else. If men are the ones who are expected by society to
make the choice, then women might be less likely to reject their
offers of marriage. Yet, the natural pliancy in women functions to
reduce stress in the marriage by making allowances for their husband's behaviour, increasing the chance of fulfilment. Although

women might willingly make these allowances, over the course of the marriage, daily experience clashes with personal belief so much that wives eventually feel that they have lost their identity, an event which, in turn, contributes to disruption later in conjugal life. Men must be initially more content with the choice of a spouse, since they are less willing to undergo a 'metamorphosis' as a concomitant to marriage. Whether it is the man or the woman making the choice, if it is not a wise one, conflict will ensue.

However, these two factors, *objectivity* and *flexibility*, are not equally strong. Research shows that the best satisfaction in marriage comes when a third party initiates or proposes the initial meeting, and this would indicate that it is not flexibility of the partners that is most important, but objectivity. A third party can often be more objective in analysing compatibility, and they might have an opinion closer to the truth than either the man or woman, *ceteris paribus*. These third parties might be relatives, friends or acquaintances. Thus, the use of *matchmakers* in the past made sense, and so leaving such matters to 'destiny' was not the conventional method of handling such a complex situation.

Since matching two people with similar characteristics is difficult, having an extended social network is a major advantage. In any setting of young people, most people will have only 1 to 3 close friends, whereas a few, perhaps about 25%, have four or more friends.[14] If A is able to associate with B, who has a considerably large network of friends, then B would have a much better chance of finding a suitable partner for A, than A would on his own. Hence, the search for a marriage partner is a much more efficient enterprise *when the aid of others is enlisted*. These potential 'matchmakers' could be constantly scrutinising eligible people for signs of compatibility. If B is particularly gregarious, he could even enlist his own friends in the search, widening the network even more. Furthermore, compared to dating services, these friends of A know more about his personality and temperament, than any simple form or survey could discern. People have a tendency to exaggerate or lie on such forms in order to make themselves more attractive. Friends, especially ones of long-standing, can assess the individual without the pretensions, and thus envision more accurate matches.

In this regard, the protocols of modern society have made it anything but easy to follow a logical, objective procedure. It is interesting that of all the myriad institutions modern society has established, not one has been created for the development of friendships, especially aimed at marriage. Instead people resort to haphazard methods, such as more or less randomly asking for a date anyone that fits in with their minimal standard of attractiveness; the office, a store, a theatre, a bar, or the street have all become places for 'romance'.[15] There is no clear boundary or time when or where it is appropriate, and when it is not, to ask for dates. Far from bringing men and women together, this inevitably creates hostility between them; women, as the ones being sought out, cannot find a place where they can be left in peace from male advances, which are sometimes quite assertive, and therefore they must erect a tough exterior as a defence. In the past, friendships were made often through more congenial methods, such as one friend referring to another friend, who in turn could refer him to another, etc. Such connections could be used whenever one liked, and relations between men and women could be more polite and less intrusive. As an adjunct to conventional means of finding dates, single people are eager to make whatever environment they inhabit more 'social' by making friends with everyone there. Widening the circle of friends obviously increases the probability that a suitable mate will be found, but drains away precious time that could profitably have been spent with the few close friends actually met through private personal connections. The deficiencies of modern social life sap energy, and consequently, fear and insecurities displace the capacity for finding meaningful relationships.

Various adjustments to personality have been made in order to increase opportunities for finding a mate. Frequent social introductions continue to be important; thus, as a way of smoothing the awkwardness between men and women, sex role behaviour has come to incorporate the traits of both sexes. In addition, improving social skills and lessening the importance of negative evaluations by peers, as well as reducing the emphasis on physical attractiveness, would increase the level of interaction by dropping barriers.[16] In recent times, in order to increase the chance of a good match, women have become not at all shy about asking men out for dates. Intrusiveness, it seems, now can work both ways. In spite of the increased social contact engendered by abandoning etiquette and more casual conversational forms, this can create greater emotional and intellectual isolation of individuals, which actually contributes to difficulty in forming intimate relationships.

As we have seen, how individuals assess others as part of an intimacy or marriage strategy is a *private process*, oftentimes more attributable to temperament than logic. Procedures can be used to determine another person's level of commitment and their interest in other members of the opposite sex. By eradicating ignorance, one can determine whether one is committed to a relationship, and a thorough examination of another person's life is therefore prudent. However, the extent to which a person takes the time to learn is dependent on patterns of energy expenditure, which can flow within, such as in the case of mental reflection, or outwardly, as in the case of socialising. Courtship requires a certain environment wherein growth can occur, where the couple seek new and significant ways to interact. In this way, men and women learn more about one another, building up the esteem that should be the bedrock of any companionate relationship. It should be apparent that although having a knowledge of form is always very profitable, honesty, integrity, devotion, caution, and perfectionism are all essential for good relationships of whatever type; no amount of strictness in protocol and formality in courtship can ever make up for a deficit of virtue. Thus, the standards of evaluation that people use are important, as are the standards that go into planning for engagement, wedding, and the first year of married life.

Since assessment is so personal, preferences must be reflected upon continually throughout the period from early puberty until the building phase of courtship. Upon entry to middle adulthood, a greater awareness of one's own and other people's preferences gains momentum in the life of the individual. Ideas about what matters and does not matter in life become more fully elucidated, reducing time and resources wasted pursuing unfruitful attachments. This not only helps in the courtship process, but establishes the operational machinery of marriage. Yet, especially for women, increasing age also brings pressures, often coming from outside the relationship, to entrust and to unify. That is, the careful evaluation of traits produced by maturity might be interrupted by larger social requirements. Whereas the former might increase the number of months of courtship, the latter might well do the opposite, making it less likely that the individual will marry a well-suited person.

This dilemma of the period of life between gaining full adult rights and losing choice, between continuing independence and sacrificing for love, was articulated by William Congreve in this way: 'Say what you will, 'tis better to be left than never to have been loved.' One could state more prosaically: 'I can't let this one go, because there might never be another chance.' The pragmatist, however, who disdains romantic notions might look at the situation somewhat differently: It is better to have married at least once, then to have never married at all. Losing one's best opportunity for intimacy due to indolence or fear is a thought that troubles even the most sensible person.

It should be obvious that a wide variety of considerations, both personal and social, must be taken into consideration before men or women accept the responsibility of marriage. We have already considered the fact that there should be emotional closeness, objectivity, flexibility, and a willingness to sacrifice. Other practical and financial matters must be taken into account, such as where the couple will live, what occupations they will have. Nonetheless, the underlying concern should be *how* does one plan for marriage, and *when* should one begin to plan.

When there is failure to achieve one's goals, many will attempt to find explanatory theories. One such common idea is that marriage has only the illusion of free choice, and in reality is actually a 'Hobson's choice', where the attributes of lifestyle, such as personality of spouse, number of children, housing, and work habits, have already been socially determined. According to this view, the *substance* of the marriage is for most not a matter of debate, but only the *timing* of its inception. The only way to avoid the pitfalls one sees in married life is to simply refrain from it all together by remaining single. However, nothing could be further from the truth. In any society, the individual has always been given choices that he might work out within the context of marriage. Certainly, there are expectations about what constitutes a 'normal' marriage, but not being mainstream is not necessarily equivalent to being deviant or anti-social. This idea of a Hobson's choice in marriage arises when *external circumstances push an individual into marrying when they are not yet emotionally or financially capable.* Pressures from parents, relatives, friends, media, or clergy might act to encourage individuals to overlook serious flaws in their partner, or to adapt their beliefs about the realities of married life. Why would there be a push to marry? We should understand that marriage is a *social* union that makes certain fundamental and unavoidable demands on people, and so married life can be used instrumentally as a way of achieving a certain envisioned lifestyle.

Thus, goals can be altered if the original pathway to intimacy is denied. For personal reasons, many women desire a stable emotional relationship with a man, and although they prize the spontaneity and allowances of unmarried romance, they might consider

marriage a reasonable solution for the problems caused by a vacil-
lating and uncooperative boyfriend. Many women rush men into
marriage because they feel the responsibilities of running a household will make their inconsiderate boyfriend more mature. Stability
in a relationship can be attained by commitment, as devotion to
another's priorities will sometimes mean relinquishing one's own.
Persistent persuasion is used, quoting statements from parents and
friends that in effect imply that marriage is unavoidable. Thus, if
the *ad hoc* relationship becomes burdensome, because of the
thoughtless and aloof behaviour of men, women will put their faith
in another, more socially-controlled type of relationship. By marrying and surrendering some of their personal freedom, men, it is
thought, will take on a new cooperative view of the world, settle
down, and deal with problems openly.

Traditionally minded women might also attempt to make a man
substantively conform to certain types of conduct, which are assumed to exist in marriage. Often, the man's problems stem from
his predilection for independence, and marriage, they naively
postulate, will force him to abandon his previously self-centred
demeanour. The thinking that motivates this approach is similar
to that used to 'break in' a recalcitrant horse, a method of condi-
tioning that involves putting the animal continually through the
paces; frequently giving instructions and pulling back on the 'reins'
are part of the 'training'.

Despite these reasons, the reality is that the push to marry is
based on an inability to establish a substitute marital relationship.
A life that emphasises autonomy and avoids commitment fosters
such situations, and so in a society where the average individual
has strongly independent feelings, marriage is used to capture or
'nail down' the inconstant, or mercurial, man or woman. There is
little doubt that belief in the Hobson's choice concept of marriage
will eventually become increasingly familiar in modern society.

Moreover, other women equivocate, not breaking off courtship or going forward into marriage, due to a mixture of conflicting reasons: It is easy keeping the status quo due to inertia; it is difficult to find another man; breaking up with potential marriage partners is embarrassing; having too many boyfriends makes one look 'cheap'; there might not be another chance at marriage.

The reality is that human behaviour is difficult, although not impossible, to change, and certainly a person who has no regard for social conventions before marriage is quite unlikely to develop a high regard for such conventions within marriage. It is reasonable to assume that *entrustment only works for people who genuinely respect it*, and fear social penalties for non-compliance. In present Western society, there is substantial lack of respect for contracts, and expecting selfish men to honour fully the marriage contract of obligations would be imprudent. We may safely say that women who marry men, without certainty how they will regard a solemn oath, could be confining themselves to years of misery.

Ignoring, or denying, key personal concepts could create a life that could very well be worse than the one had by remaining single. Is it better to have no ideals, but to be married, or to have strong ideals, but to be alone? This is a question that can only be answered by the individual, as long as he or she has taken into account the dangers of disregarding either marriage or idealism. Nonetheless, creating an idealised model of one's potential mate can sometimes be a deterrent to settling for compromise situations; no one can be expected to fit perfectly into one's conceptions. Too many unrealistic requirements about the ideal spouse's personality will make difficult the marriage discovery process. However, there should never be any restriction on *essential* requirements about character, even if such requirements are constructed in such as way that one never makes a suitable match.

To summarise, we have noted that people will deepen a friendship based on mutual enhancement, when they believe there is future entrustment and constancy. The process of courtship provides the path to taking this deepening to its logical conclusion, namely that of marriage, but it does not imply that the individual presently has the *capacity* to marry. Discovering whether a potential mate is willing to be committed to a relationship is not difficult, but the ascertainment might be time-consuming. We can see in higher-ranking areas of life that *time* is the most important and yet least controlled resource. In order to do things properly, the individual must have enough time to learn about procedures, collect information, and make credible decisions. That being the case, clearly, *everyone who intends to marry, should plan for this event as early as possible*. However, to build a married life that endures long into the future, personal factors must be taken into account, such as character, temperament, tastes, beliefs, emotions; inevitably, the process of 'marriage' must be obeyed: Exploring, evaluation, building, and execution. The reasons why someone would marry are many, nevertheless, they can be distilled into several all-important categories. Within the evolution of a successful relationship, it is essential to continue knowing one's own interests; to understand why one needs a companion to meet these goals; to know how to communicate one's desires effectively; and to have a willingness to sacrifice. These principles are reasonable, and have yet to be proven wrong.

In developing a view of marriage, one should be aware that there are factors that operate for and against marriage, which affect the process of building a relationship. In European history, four motivations have emerged that have encouraged marriage. Firstly, the emotional well-being and happiness of family life; secondly, the social prestige, acceptance, and rank that marriage confers; thirdly, the satisfaction in having children for economic and legacy reasons; fourthly, the maximisation of domestic, financial, and other pragmatic material conditions. Obtaining reliable information about the context in which these motivations occurred difficult, as little is known about the personal reasons why people married in the past.

Unfortunately, scholarship lacks in-depth surveys of pre-20th century populations, making it difficult to analyse the first two motivations. However, the third and fourth are easier to examine as they are largely utilitarian, and therefore recordable. For example, having children for economic reasons is apparent in societies where they are considered useful in production.

On the other hand, there are basically two obstacles to marriage. One is a lack of interest in, and attraction to, the opposite sex, a fundamental force that is not easily explained by environmental or sociological factors, with evidence to show that it is, to an extent, genetically determined. The other reason, of less but by no means trivial significance, is a lack of income and savings. In traditional societies where the pull is toward marriage, once the man has enough money saved and a good job, he will be ready for marriage. In modern society, the cultural pull is toward *bachelorhood* (where the individual maintains his freedom, casual lifestyle, and spontaneity), so a good salary would almost compel him to remain single. It should be emphasised, that absence of money, or a surplus of it, is not inherently positive or negative, for these and other aspects *interact* with various attributes.

As we stated earlier, many factors influence the male-female intimate relationship, and the axiomatic difficulty of reconciling them all makes people forget that successful marriages must be *created by design*. It is sometimes thought that, for all the pieces to fall into place, it must be great fortune indeed. Nevertheless, this approach ignores the fact that people can *grow* intellectually and emotionally, and the multiplicity of considerations does not render the individual impotent in making decisions about his life. One has to seriously determine what combination of characteristics one actually possesses. For example: I am the gregarious type, honest, with simple wants, but possessive—or,—I am well-off financially, self-centred to an extent, but still capable of empathy and change. Similarly, one has to determine the characteristics of other people.

Somehow, some way, people do try to make sense out of all of these factors, and although it might be difficult, it is certainly not impossible to carefully assess all of them. Moreover, where the individual assiduously collects wisdom on the subject of marriage, he will always be empowered, by obtaining a fresh perspective on the dynamics of relationships.

Completing the search for a potential partner who has desirable traits, a good disposition, constancy and commitment, is relatively easy, when compared to the long, futile struggle of trying to keep a blend of mismatched ingredients from turning into a farrago. Although the quest is difficult, many intelligent and sincere people will find the right approach to the challenge, one that is consistent with their personality, their desire for independence, and their emotional needs. This approach might include other individuals who can assist a young man or woman in putting together a tangible scheme that would fulfill diverse personal needs, although there is only one person who ultimately has the final authority to render a decision, and so only one who must take responsibility for that decision. 'We should marry to please ourselves, not other people', would be a good motto.[17]

Further, as men and women have been meeting, courting, and marrying for many centuries, societies have collected and preserved these experiences in cultural concepts. For many people, culture is an important, perhaps the most important, factor in resolving the competing ideas swirling about the issue of marriage. All European cultures pull together and circulate several basic ideas pertinent to family life. We can say that, based upon observation, that it is nearly universally believed that marriage should be delayed until the couple's economic conditions have reached some minimal standard, and most are also willing to concede that marriage should take place between a minimum age and a maximum age. But there are many 'dissenters'. Some people advocate marriage only when the couple are certain of emotional compatibility; others claim a couple can marry even before they are settled on career paths; and yet others maintain that marriage should be avoided whenever possible, with celibacy as a better form of life. The forces that motivate a person to maintain these divergent attitudes vary in intensity, and are the result of a complex mixture of temperament, history, and social necessity.

Thus, the community puts forward, in its historically based cultural assemblage of ideas, many principles that can often compensate for individual ignorance, which can aid the individual in making a decision about marriage. This removes part of the burden of evaluating complex situations, but at the same time, does not take away the responsibility of correct action. Although the predisposition to fraternise with the opposite sex is certainly different from one person to the next, and varies in relation to the degree of extroversion, a culture, in some cases, might impose itself to form a *false disposition*, an incorrectly perceived 'innate' tendency. A culture is, of course, the composite of individual temperaments, and its rules and practises are normally consistent with consensus opinion. However, even in the most racially homogenous nation, not *everyone* has the same temperament, and the culture might act to force those who deviate to conform to larger practises. As a result, we must be careful not to confuse *advice* with *directives*; we seek wisdom about the forces that stand in the way, or catalyse the move to, *connubium*. Society might 'expect' everyone to marry, but people who never marry should not be penalised. Such an 'expectation' can often 'clear the way' for those seeking marriage, and facilitate major changes in life, as long as opportunities for marriage with a suitable partner exist within one's peer group. It is then easier to make the allowance for a spouse into one's home environment and career. A personal need to marry, through an intensification of feeling for friendship, love, or companionship, must of course be present, although one must also guard against these feelings being overly influenced by culture.

We should reiterate, for the sake of prudence, that the ultimate force that guides us in life is our own God-given Free Will. Every other force should come under the category of 'influence', not 'cause'. There are two situations where this principle is violated, i.e., when influences become causes: When one deliberately makes oneself pliable to social forces due to a fear of losing status, and when one cannot refuse a social demand due to fear of major retribution. Thus, as long as the individual maintains his independent thinking, and there is no undue coercion, the success or failure of an action is ultimately that individual's responsibility.

Marriage is, therefore, a precarious adventure with great risks, but also with tremendous rewards. Whenever human beings are faced with such a situation, the tendency is to either bear down and meet the challenge, or to retreat into over-simplifications and fantasies. Accordingly, we should address this issue concerning the history of a great continent: Have Europeans, on the whole, made intelligent use of the positive resources that they have had at their disposal, such as the wisdom obtained from tradition, and the advice and assistance of more knowledgeable individuals? Further we ask: Have European cultures protected and facilitated the individual's efforts to follow his own path in the matter of marriage? To answer these questions, we must realise that our European ancestors carefully contemplated and weighed the issues of personality, friendship, individuality, social influences, and culture, thus producing doctrines and processes that have been passed across many generations. Let us now study, objectively, the quality of these doctrines, and the feasibility of these processes.

Chapter 5

Traditional Wisdom

*O*bservation tells us that the pursuit of advantage is probably the most powerful factor in human existence. How to accomplish this is dependent on an individual's skills, experiences, talents, as well on the social and natural environment. One person might be highly ambitious and motivated to work, but have few opportunities available. Another person might be poorly motivated, yet have numerous opportunities opening up all around him. Obviously, motivation and occasion are not always related, but few would say that they have no interest in gaining something tangible from life.

The means to success vary by time and place; however, most people have some knowledge what is required in order to obtain money, power, status, and, ultimately, *gratification*, within the secure enclosure of marriage. As European history demonstrates, to make headway in life a chain of major events must be followed—education must come first, followed by establishing an occupation, then accumulating significant savings, then followed by increased social status. Although it was only in the early 19th century that this chain of events became formalised, where 'institutions' arose to meet the need for clear fulfilment of each stage, the deliberate enactment of personal progress has existed probably since the beginning of the human race. We should not make the mistake of believing that people in the past simply moved from one household to another as part of a subsistence strategy. The farmer in Spain or Norway went through the same stages of development

as the modern stock-broker in New York or London. Both cultures
are linked in a basic way by the desire to achieve a transcendent
contentment. The difference between these ages lies in the *intensity*
of experience of each stage, not in the *nature* of experience.

Thus, the final factor in the chain of life's milestones—contentment—could not be possible unless full use is made of social engagement, education, and career, in the establishment and mainte-
nance of love. We should appreciate the fact that this linkage, of
the profoundly *physical* with the profoundly *emotional*, is buried
deep in European psyche. In spite of the recent creation of support
institutions, neither the desire for true love nor these factors leading to contentment is modern. What our generation might call
'quaint' or 'cherished and dear' feelings about one's spouse are
neither recent 'romantic' ideas, nor are they unattainable. The
container of ideas we call 'tradition' has much wisdom to give us,
if we take the time to examine it.

For example, the ancient Romans unabashedly extolled the
virtues of marriage, looking upon life-long union as indicative of
stability and fidelity. The giving of life to such important concepts
was rewarded by the community, and even in some cases, by the
gods, as in the myth of Philemon and Baucis. The Hebrews also
knew about the importance of emotional attachment, as Ecclesias-
tes 9:9 (NIV) says to 'Enjoy life with your wife, whom you love, all
the days of this meaningless life that God has given you under the
sun.' Following Judaic traditions, the Christian Church from the
beginning expected only the most caring and empathetic relationship between husbands and wives. Note that this expectation had
nothing to do with material considerations, either before or after
the fact. Emotional fulfilment was openly promoted as the focus
of marriage, as when St Paul, in Ephesians 5:28 (NIV), enjoins
husbands to love their wives as 'their own bodies. He who loves his
wife loves himself.' Traditional Christianity, despite its praise of
celibacy, recognised that extraordinary happiness could be

achieved in marriage as well, as we can see in the lives of many canonised men and women throughout the last two millennia. Some of the more major figures were Paula (347-404), Elizabeth of Hungary (1207-1231), Frances of Rome (1384-1440), Nicholas von Flüe (1417-1487), Joan de Lestonnac (1556-1640). Besides these saints, many intellectuals, poets, painters, musicians, composers also had happy marriages. John Donne (1572-1631), whose poems and sermons are considered some of the best of the 17th century, openly credited his wife for his emotional strength and inspiration. One of the most charming descriptions of domestic tranquillity comes from the life of composer Heinrich Schütz (1585-1672). Although an author of exquisite sacred pieces, and totally imbued in mellifluity, it was said that he 'never knew or heard a more lovely sound or song, than when he heard the voice or word of his precious wife.' 'She cared for him daily . . . when he came home from his work she was overjoyed to see him, and ran with happiness to greet him'.[18] Both Donne and Schütz lost their wives tragically early and neither remarried, which as a pragmatic matter, was rather unusual for their time. Fortunately, both used their respective losses as an inspiration to make the love they had felt personally resonate through the word, voice and instrument.

No one can regard the warm thoughts of literate people of the past without admitting that affection was indeed common, and not something abnormal, unusual, or strange.[19] That these types of loving unions were praised by contemporaries shows both high regard for affection between spouses, and the absence of concern about uxoriousness.[20] The reason for our lack of knowledge about such marriages is more attributable to the paucity of detailed biographies describing the private lives of ordinary men and women, rather than a pessimistic view of romance. Ironically, the people that we know most about—the kings, queens, dukes, duchesses, and other high-born nobility and aristocracy—often had the worst marriages, suffering through loveless relationships that were the product of arranged unions. Perhaps this is one reason why some think of the past as being wrapped in cold emotional desolation.

Modern writers have often denied the possibility that our ancestors generally achieved contentment from love; academia has a remarkably dichotomised view of the relations between men and women, where, to put it simply, the past was 'pragmatic', the present is 'romantic'.[21] For example, one author states that compared to the pre-industrial age of our ancestors, society of our time looks at the married couple not as a 'simple unit of production, but as a focus of affection and solidarity'.[22] From the point of view of the modern age, the history of the Western world could be reduced to simplistic metaphors of winter and summer: A cold, sterile pre-modern folk, marrying only for money; and passionate modern individuals, where romance is the overriding factor. Yet, this view is erroneous, and the truth may be that people of the past might have put *more emphasis on love* than modern people. To look at past marriage in merely economic terms grossly underestimates the *value of affection*. It is true that material aspects were perhaps more of an anxious concern than in our day, but this does not mean that fondness, and deep emotional satisfaction, were irrelevant. Many today see the two issues as mutually exclusive: Either a couple is materially orientated, or they are romantically orientated.[23]

Thus, our ancestors certainly did not view marriage as necessarily lacking in affection or thoughtfulness; most would certainly have been shocked if told that affection does not have to be at the centre of the ideal or proper marital relationship. Further, because they would have criticised a 'love-only' highly romanticised relationship as reckless, they should not be condemned as unfeeling pragmatists. As respect, cooperation, consideration—all key ingredients of affection—were expected of, and experienced by, family members, friends, and relatives, to have it lacking between a husband and wife would have been strange indeed.[24]

In the very long history of Western civilisation, it is fair to say

that there is *consistency*: Themes of money, occupation, matching
of personality, and opportunity have all played major roles in the
decision to marry. Emotional, along with material concerns lay at
the heart of our ancestors' male-female relations, though, for very
different reasons than the ones posited by historians. Status was
often matched due to a conscious desire for similarity, but personalities were intended to be complementary. Hence, in previous
generations, greater external or public emphasis was put on material concerns, compared to emotional compatibility. The extent of
dissimilarity between people in material factors was larger than in
morals or traits, and so there was a prevalence of discussions that
attempted to reconcile differences in status, rather than character.

Traditional wisdom was inherited by each generation and 'taken
to heart', some people being more influenced, others less. There
was enough similarity within and between regions so that a European set of 'norms' can be constructed, although customs varied
from one region to the next, and were sometimes quite untypical.
In trying to understand individual dynamics, whether a town,
village, district, or territory was part of this standard is largely irrelevant, as local norms are oftentimes the product of an ethnic
disposition—the 'spirit' of a people—which is in contention with
specific challenges. Other customs, however, cannot be explained
in such a way, and are likely the result of a greater than normal
variation in inherent genetic disposition. Thus, the 'character' of
a local ethnic group emerges from a matrix of manifold influences,
a cultural assemblage that is part economic, part demographic, part
organisational, part genetic, and part undetermined.

We must therefore determine the extent to which human beings
deny the influence of external forces, i.e., the extent to which they
freely and consciously *choose their own course*. If people largely
allow external forces to shape their destiny, then finding high cor-
relations in history is likely; if not, then it would be nearly impossible to predict communal behaviour, and the work of scholars would

be of a different type. All science revolves around the simple fact that in order to establish dynamics, there must be the ability to see *patterns* in data. In studying the past, clear evidence of autonomous behaviour, whether by the individual or some social unit, is difficult to obtain, and so assumptions about 'similarity' and 'diversity' among cultures must be clarified. It is entirely appropriate, and indeed necessary, to carefully classify the manifestations of a phenomenon, and note the apparent 'differences' between two regions or communities by putting them into two different 'categories'. But to reduce the number of categories, whether for the sake of expediency or following some partisan ideological programme, is a mistake. If one is trying to prove the existence of a phenomenon, e.g., that economic activity has a decisive impact on human behaviour, then one might be tempted to classify observations in a certain way (by putting them into the 'same' category, or two or more 'different' categories) so as to further a theory.

Success in proving the decisive impact of any physical phenomenon necessarily reduces the influence of that most basic, irreducible factor called *Free Will*. In studying any society, we must determine whether people make a choice due to an unquantifiable internal force (i.e. Free Will); due to identifiable internal forces, such as social concerns, ideology, apathy, habit; due to some other force external to the specific problem; due to a lack of an alternative, i.e. externally imposed 'choice'; due to ignorance about the alternatives. We touched upon this issue earlier in relation to the question of whether a marital union was by fate, or by choice. If people's actions are governed mostly by Free Will, then theories about the 'inevitability' of choice due to economics or culture are seriously jeopardised. For example, it is a well-known phenomenon that economic considerations prompted couples to have many children in pre-modern agricultural areas (i.e. high fertility). It would be a major mistake, though, to simply assume that whatever variations in fertility we see are due mainly to economic considerations, or even worse due to bias, to dismiss the fertility difference between two economically *identical* regions as 'negligible', when that difference might in some other context be called 'significant'. The fact is that a couple might *consciously* choose to have a large number of children, and might *consciously* reject advanced procedures that would increase agricultural productivity, as well as their financial standing. Contemporary accounts sometimes make a point of saying that the squalor that was witnessed was as much the result of indolence of people, as that of exploitation, inflation, unemployment, or usury.[25] However, the cause for the social situation was usually left open to interpretation.

As a consequence of these issues, we must make cautious use of the information derived from various, though not necessarily competing, sources, such as census data, parish information, school materials, proverbs, legends, and personal statements. Some are actual facts, some are ideals, others are counter-ideals. We should bear in mind that we cannot look at these observations with the same reliability as numerical evidence. What might be perceptible to the scientist in a statistical sense might not be so to an observer, even if trained. Further, the necessity to cite something in one's report might be dependent on the event's moral qualities. One describes a place or situation when something goes wrong, rather than when something goes right, and chances are that the authors of historical documents, on the whole, overemphasise the bad and neglect the good. Differences in the size of the community might engender divergent rules about interpretation of data; rural communities might be held to different standards than urban ones. Also, the men who wrote the reports had to match the expectations of the time in order to maintain their social and governmental position—they might be ideological 'purists' who make accurate descriptions, but only within a limited scope of observation. Defects in information might be attributed to the interviewee, as much as the interviewer. In addition, lying, boasting, exaggerations might have been prevalent, perhaps as a way to denigrate a culture or family and so elevating one's own.[26] Systematic analysis has come slowly in scholarship; researchers converged their mental and physical resources on things that they understood, things that interested them, or things that they were assigned to observe. The level of error can, therefore, be high in 'anthropological' reports, leading to false impressions that can persist for many years.[27]

Thus, because of the importance of separating free choice from forced choice, in considering history we cannot overstress the importance of acknowledging the considerable *diversity* of family situations, whilst also paying attention to the *similarity* within a culture. Yet, human beings have a tendency to reduce diversity as a way of simplifying a problem. Although our ancestors in Europe shared fundamental moral precepts, to the point where we can confidently say that certain attitudes were universal, other beliefs were adiaphorous (having no clear moral impact), which varied according to processes of the natural environment, individual temperament, collective temperament, and challenges from outside the community. Despite these profundities, many modern authors have preferred simplistic, and so misleading statements: 'Wives were beasts of burden', 'girls were not wanted', 'clans had a strong hold on their members'. Such factors might have existed locally or regionally, but again, they do not necessarily capture the deeper 'spirit' of a people.

It is reasonable to conclude, that one should assess all the facts before attempting to consolidate nations or regions into one category. One can, and *should*, consolidate when it is required or efficient, but only when there is also adequate justification; objective researchers have discovered, upon investigation, cases where such procedures were unwarranted.[28]

Interestingly, one of the most common examples of overgeneralising cultural values is found in relation to marriage. Did previous generations judge this process as largely *voluntary* or *involuntary*?

The prevailing attitude among modern laypeople is that it was the latter, that men and especially women were often forced to marry against their will, having to do so in order to meet society's expectations of fulfilment of mother or father roles, to provide children for society's well-being, to become a productive, and honourable member of the community. That *some* were forced, coerced, or cajoled into matrimony is beyond question, but there is no evidence that, at least in Christian European civilisation, there was any *long-term, widely-accepted 'duty' to marry*. In reference to our discussion about the modern tendency to mischaracterise cultural values, we may wonder whether this idea is some sort of psychological projection from our own age onto the lives of our ancestors.

Let us examine the purported pressures to marry that might have existed, which can be divided into four main categories: Cultural duty, pregnancy, family obligation, and economic necessity. The first is one of the easiest to ascertain, and it is the easiest to dismiss as a major factor. We know that traditionally the Roman Catholic Church emphasised the absolute right of the individual to refuse marriage, and the absolute right to marry whomever he or she chose. The Council of Trent's *Decree Concerning the Reform of Matrimony* made a forceful statement about the illegitimate linkage of financial imperatives, social prestige and marriage:

> *Worldly inclinations and desires very often so blind the mental vision of temporal lords and magistrates, that by threats and ill usage they compel men and women who live under their jurisdiction, especially the rich or those who expect a large inheritance, to contract marriage against their will with those whom these lords or magistrates propose to them. Wherefore, since it is something singularly execrable to violate the freedom of matrimony, and equally execrable that injustice should come from those from whom justice is expected, the holy council commands all, of whatever rank, dignity and profession they may be, under*

penalty of anathema to be incurred ipso facto, that do in any manner whatever, directly or indirectly, compel their subjects or any others whomsoever in any way that will hinder them from contracting marriage freely.[29]

Not only does this restate long-standing Church moral tenets on marriage, it also indicates that there were serious enough lapses to justify issuing this statement. Of course, if such restrictions were promulgated for the high-born, then they would apply to all the lesser classes as well. The latest revision of Canon Law is also passionate in its condemnation of any kind of 'persuasion' which reduces a person's choices, with the only option being to marry an individual that has been put forward by a party in control.

A marriage is invalid if it is entered into due to force or grave fear inflicted from outside the person, even when inflicted unintentionally, which is of such a type that the person is compelled to choose matrimony in order to be freed from it.
(Canon 1103).[30]

The specific meaning of 'force' or 'grave fear' is not given in this document, but one could legitimately define this as any kind of duress, including interminable nagging by a parent if it causes depression or other significant distress that can only be alleviated by acceding to the persistent demands. The validity of a marriage might, therefore, be a function of the subjective opinion as to the nature of the 'force'. Additionally, the Church was, and continues to be, so concerned with this freedom of marriage choice, that even *unintentional* coercion makes the union invalid. As marriage is one of the most important decisions one could make in one's life, if not the most important, then achieving happiness and contentment is paramount; any kind of coercion is truly unconscionable.

Thus, the cultures of Europe, as they are derived in large part from biblical teaching, the canons of the Roman Catholic Church, the catechism, and the writings of the early Church Fathers, *must have promoted an unequivocal adherence to the principle of Free Will in matrimonial matters*.

Besides the loud, unhesitant proclamations of the universal and powerful Church, which found their way into all parishes, it is clear that the common sayings of European peoples about marriage, love, husband, wife, and children, as compiled by Meider (1986), exhibit a sincere concern with correct individual choice. If undue cultural pressure to marry had been common over the last two to three hundred years, when these expressions were formed and used, then certainly the adages of the folk would have revealed the true situation. Yet, there are few statements which mention external impositions; in fact, there is quite commonly an urging to *forestall* or *forego* marriage, showing that if anyone were at fault, it was the individual who chose improperly due to lack of forethought.

As for pragmatic factors, we can see that *pre-marital pregnancy* did not hasten marriage, as pre-nuptially conceived births were fairly uncommon, and illegitimacy rates, with some exceptions, were low until the 20th century, indicating adherence to traditional mores.[31] More difficult to gauge is the desire to maintain the *family lineage*, but if folk sayings are an indication of disposition, then we can say that such influence was not overwhelming, although certainly it was greater than that passed on by the community.

As for the effects of the *economy* on the decision to marry, here indeed there is evidence of conditions that work against early marriage, and favour late marriage. For example, when real wages in England are compared to crude marriage rates in the period 1551 to 1851, we find that the tendency to marry was predicated on changes in the economy.[32] France followed a similar pattern, where a negative correlation existed between grain prices and marriage rates in the 19th century.[33] However, in England there was a thirty-year lag on average between a change in wages and a change in marriage rate. This might be the result of a whole generation experiencing a declining economy, for example, and then entering this into the cultural 'record', where the next generation reacts to it. However, from this reliable data we do draw an important insight into the internal disposition of Western Europeans. As we do not see any evidence of *inflexibility on the upward or downward side* throughout this period, we conclude that people were not *innately* more inclined to marry, or not to marry. Further, personal choice still prevailed in many cases. Although economic factors clearly influenced the decision to marry, *there were many who went against the trend*. In fact, during the steep declines in income of the period from about 1751 to about 1771, *most* people in England went ahead and married 'foolishly', and during the periods of improving economy of 1625 to 1671, and 1820 to 1840, *most* failed to react swiftly and forwent marriage 'unwisely'. These periods of counter-trend behaviour (the 'lag' mentioned above), when so many people quite deliberately married in the midst of a slumping economy, do not diminish the strong larger conventional trend. Hence, the economy's influence in the decision to marry, albeit substantial, *was by no means absolute*, and the exercise of true individual motivation was evident.

Let us now look more closely at the economic and other external influences that affected the individual's ability to translate into reality the ideals that he held in his mind about companionship and independence. As we do not have any objective indicator of the 'willingness' to marry, we must extract whatever information we can from the indicators that we do have. In research on the marital practises of the past, the emphasis is usually on two dependent variables: Average age of marriage and celibacy rates. Age of marriage and celibacy rates are widely available, going back to at least the 17th century. These figures, in association with other social and economic statistics, can enlighten us as to how individuals evaluated the life engendered by matrimony.

The current model of marriage practises in the traditional era stems in part from the work of John Hajnal;[34] the concepts proposed in the 1960s have been revised as various anomalies continue to be considered.[35] Building his theory on Malthusian ideas, Hajnal asserted that there is a 'zone' of low nuptiality in Europe, northwest of a line drawn from Trieste, Italy to St Petersburg, Russia. He believed that this division, which arose between the 16th and 17th centuries, was based on a tradition that required a newly married couple to form a *separate independent household*. The performance of the economy was thus a critical factor in determining the age of marriage, and the basis for a household, and in one sense for 'love', was financial. Europeans had become inured to achieving a certain lifestyle and were reluctant to fall below that standard; indeed, they wanted to progress to a higher level than the previous generation. People maintained, paradoxically, a type of 'American dream' long before there was an America.

'Low nuptiality' is one way of saying permanent celibacy, and historical surveys show the persistent and widespread, though not constant, occurrence of celibacy throughout Europe. Because of this diversity of marriage patterns, scholars have been unable to cite some overriding cultural factor to explain low nuptiality. Instead, the economic situation, with similar variety of local conditions superimposed on regional and international trends, is often implicated in the propensity to marry. *Economic developments affect occupations and living standards, which in turn affects the need and desire for marriage.* Traditionally, for women, marriage conflicted with employment as a servant; for men, a greater involvement with their occupation, such as working long hours, travelling, and socialising, etiolated relations with women.

Moreover, demographic factors were often instrumental in keeping people away from marriage; the cities provided diversions and entertainment for many people, whilst offering better living conditions and alternative family structures for many men and women

of the lower classes. We can see these situations in an analysis of
death records for a parish in Warsaw, Poland for the period of 1760
to 1801.[36] The percent who remained single until death increased
during this period. For men, the percent single increased from
about 8% to 24%; for women, the figures are more erratic, but
rising from about 4% to 11%. These are high figures by our current
Western standards, especially for men.

Census records give us a similar picture, showing even higher
rates of celibacy. However, the city was in the past a fairly volatile
demographic entity, and we should be careful in assessing census
records as these point to a particular point in time. People can
temporarily settle in a locale, which might significantly change the
balance of single to married. A 1791 census of the same parish
found that about 22% of men and women over age 50 were single,
but this included large numbers of tradesmen, senators, servants
and others who had come on the occasion of the debates in the
Great Parliament held in 1788 to 1792. This underlines the difficulties inherent in obtaining accurate celibacy rates, and death record
analysis might be somewhat more accurate in assessing proportions. In addition, other local conditions were in effect that might
make the rates for one city very different from other similar sized
cities. The rates for women in this parish resemble that of smaller
towns in Western Europe, as higher proportions of women living
in the larger towns and cities were permanently celibate.[37]

We might ask the question: Why would some cultures stress
caution in relation to marriage, as preserved in their aphorisms,
when they undoubtedly had periods *when married life was considered rewarding?* This positivism would have reigned during times
of lower mortality, economic growth, and older age of first marriage. Perhaps most people had a good opinion of the *concept* of
marriage, which they attempted to implement, but might have had
a poor opinion of the implementation of marriage that they saw in
their own communities. It was this high valuation of the concept

of 'Marriage', that made people react quite negatively to the 'marriage' of everyday life when they witnessed *others* misuse this institution. Since a good marriage has always been difficult to come by, people might have been somewhat harsh about marriage, reflecting a very common saying, 'better safe than sorry'.

To address the question we posed earlier, as to whether Europeans properly employed various external agencies, we can conclude that the people of the past indeed had the great ability to make up their own minds about marriage, utilising culturally derived knowledge. Within the traditional realm, there was an *expectation* that the individual would carefully deliberate this decision, and not rush into it on account of the push from mother or father, or the pull of infatuation, status, intimacy, or financial advancement. Thus, historically, the wisdom that tradition bestowed were accepted as *guidelines*, but not as *dictates*. Many people did not resign themselves to the 'forces of fate' when it came to the choice of marriage partner, but attempted to forge their own individual path utilising customary knowledge that assisted them in interpreting economic developments.

However, in the early stages of the Industrial Revolution, many no longer followed conventions, and the importance of cities resulted in the declining value of traditional structures and amenities. Europeans sensed a growing rift between not only each other, but between their ideals and their achievements. The first signs of this antagonism are apparent in the domestic domain, where the demands of a complex economy, migration, and standards of living affected the pursuit of intimacy in courtship and marriage patterns.

Therefore, let us examine further this segmentation as it appeared in the family and community. In relation to the forces that influence the ideals of love and independence, and so ultimately the decision to marry, we shall move from the *outer spheres* of the individual's life, that of religion, community, economy, and business, to the *inner sphere*, that of the family.

Chapter 6

Personal Attitudes and Pragmatic Customs

*C*hanges to the economic structure in the early Industrial Age fostered a view that traditional concepts, far from being beneficent, were an unnecessary hindrance to the newly emerging goals of modern life. Let us investigate this intriguing period when macrosocial factors, such as *finances, occupation,* and *government,* openly challenged important microsocial components, such as *ideals, emotions,* and *family structure.*

We start by looking at nineteenth century Spain, as examined in Reher (1991), which exhibits practises and principles that were fairly typical across Europe in the early Industrial period. Some of the main themes we have already seen, others are more personal: Dependence on inheritance money; occupational limitations on female servants; marriage market inequalities; and death-related opportunity effects, were all significant factors, and prioritised in that order. In general, these factors held better for females, and for explaining celibacy rather than age of marriage. Male and female celibacy rates were geographically coincident, ranging from about 3% in the central portions, to highs of 15% and more in the northern coastal region, parts of the eastern coast, and the south. Inheritance practises coincided with the propensity to marry: The more impartible the inheritance practise, the later the marriage age, and the greater the percentage of those who remain celibate. Unable to obtain the funds for married life, many had little choice but to remain celibate, either living with their families, with non-related housemates, or in a domestic service situation. In the last case, it is not surprising that the more girls who worked as servants, the later the marriage and more celibacy. As marriage between servants was often not possible, a person in such an occupation was limited in this regard relative to other occupations. Moreover, the lower the male-female ratio, i.e. fewer males per females, the lower female nuptiality. Thus, out-migration, from the region to other areas, resulted in many women being left without a match. There is a significant interaction between impartible inheritance and sex-ratio, indicating men left the area if they could not inherit, a situation which created an imbalance in the sex-ratio.

Economic factors were responsible to a large extent for the changes in the last theme mentioned above, that of mortality. Poor work conditions and high population density in cities were undoubtedly responsible for many unnecessary deaths. Hence, the toll that the new modern economy exacted on health and emotional well-being must have affected personal psychology: it dampened enthusiasm for life and love. Bearing this in mind, it is puzzling, however, why people in Spain were *more* likely to marry if the incidence of mortality was *higher*. Clearly, certain factors *overrode the emotional reaction to social disruption*. Possibly seeing an opportunity to marry when a husband or wife died, an individual could, in this way, raise his or her status, and so to an extent increasing the feeling of independence. To put it another way, a man might never have married, had not another man died and made his wife 'available' again in the marriage market.

This association between death rates and nuptiality might not entirely be based on personal financial considerations; individuals might have seen *overpopulation*, in the community and the home, as another threat to their independence. Society has always been understandably sensitive to changes in its size, and has found ways to control it. Before the use of artificial contraception, the only reliable way to control fertility was through marriage practise.

Indeed, 'the classic regulatory mechanism among west European populations of the early modern period was marriage'.[38] The special demands of larger society were not lost on most individuals, as the economic welfare of the individual, and to a large extent his *autonomy*, was consciously tied to the welfare of the whole society. When death rates declined, the annual increase in the population would be higher, and the only way to stop the population from reaching unmanageable levels was by delaying marriage.

The evidence tends to support this thesis, for it shows that *mortality was connected to celibacy rates in early modern Europe*. We see that in the 18th century an improvement in death rates was met by a delay in and abandonment of marriage. In the period from 1700 to 1880, the celibacy rate in France rose steadily and peaked for women at nearly 15% in 1820, and for men at around 10% in 1840. For women the low in 1700 was about 5%, and in 1880, it was 11%; for men the figures were respectively 5% and 8%. These changes could be attributed to a form of population control, where the birth rate was lowered as a result of *higher celibacy and late marriage in order to compensate for lower mortality*. Therefore, microsocial measures such as these served effectively to stabilise the population and the economy. Population growth was managed through various mechanisms as a way of avoiding overuse of resources including land, the most important of which was delaying marriage as a way of reducing the number of births per woman.

Thus, across Europe, *changes in marriage practise resulted from changes in living conditions*. It would appear that limitations were imposed when people were very conscious that a rise in population would endanger the welfare of all, a state of affairs present in late 19th century Ireland, France, and other parts of the continent. Even with impressive images of whole communities starving because of uncontrolled fertility, people were probably more conscious of the dangers of overpopulation in the far more relevant 'region' of the household. On this social scale, standard of living is more important than possible early death, which is seen only as the most dire consequence of unregulated population growth.

Our conclusion is that, although affected to an extent by the possible dangers to the community of overpopulation, men and women were chiefly concerned with a 'microsocial' aspect, that of attaining higher quality of life, thus disregarding traditional concepts. In cultures where opportunities for asset accumulation were limited, it is possible that there was greater emphasis on judicious expenditure planning within marriage. The poor accumulation of assets at the beginning of marriage was probably linked with having a lower echelon job (a job other than artisan or merchant, for example), which in turn made current income meagre. Further, as savings were generally not available, the family had to be very parsimonious in its spending habits. But more than anything else, a married couple had to pay close attention to their reproductive activities. The principle involved, unlike others concerning trade or finance, was actually so simple that even the most uneducated could understand it. Every child required more food, and in order to avoid economic strain, that child should work to feed himself or herself. A very young child is obviously incapable of self-care, but once a child reached an age where he or she could help in the family enterprise, then income (of whatever form) would increase, and another child could be added to the household. A clearly defined period of separation between births is of critical importance, with the goal of never having more mouths to feed than could be provided for. Consequently, a woman marrying later, but having the same interval between births and the same age of final birth would have, indeed must have, a *lower* fertility than a woman marrying early. In this case, the cultural factor of timing, or birth spacing, is more important than exogenous economic forces.

Although we are looking at marriage across a wide expanse of time, there is no doubt couples practised various means of controlling their fertility, including periodic abstinence, coitus interruptus, and, infrequently, abortion and infanticide, the most reliable method was through the *adjustment of the age of marriage*.

Thus, marriage age is a regulatory mechanism or fertility 'governor' preventing overpopulation which causes a lower quality of life and, more uncommonly, higher death rates. The governor's viability is based, however, on two premises. One is that men and women in times of potential or real material distress delay marriage, because they do not have the financial means to establish a household. The other is that couples who marry later, do not take measures to accelerate or decelerate the pace of births; that is, the spacing of children within marriage is the same, regardless of marriage age. The first premiss is very common throughout history, the second is more problematic. It is assumed in the latter premiss that people do not use any other form of contraception except abstinence, and that given a certain natural fecundity, babies will 'come when they will come'.

The idea that marriage age strongly governs fertility is weakened by the observation that the equal spacing rule is subject to many exceptions, where couples do not leave to chance the number of children they eventually will produce, but have a specific *target* in mind. This target is based upon the minimal quality of life a child should have, the amount of emotional gratification each child brings, and the amount of additional income of each additional child. Historically, couples have had reasons to purposefully abstain from sexual intercourse in order to reduce the possibility of pregnancy. For example, sometimes a *rise* in child mortality was met with a *decline* in fertility not a gain, demonstrating a definite control of fertility *within* marriage. This was the case in the English village of Colyton where childlessness for women marrying below age 35 went from 8% to about 20% in the period from 1560 to 1770.[39] It is plausible that couples might not have wanted children in high mortality periods, in order to avoid the almost inevitable heartbreak of losing a child, even if it meant being deprived of valuable labour on the farm. Emotion has had a key role to play in this area of fertility, as in many others associated with marriage.

Other anomalies occur. There are instances where, for example, marriage is late, yet where fertility is also high. In areas where men and women have adequate work before marriage, they might be able to *accumulate substantial savings*, so that if they were to marry late, their financial position would allow for more children than if they married early. Thus, an early marrying couple would have 100 units of currency saved, and a late marrying couple might have 200 units. If each wanted to spend the same amount per child, then the late marrying couple would have more children than the early marrying one, if nature cooperated. However, this would only apply if the woman in question did not work, or worked little in outside employment after marriage. This is, indeed, the pattern for industrialised societies, where it was not uncommon for females to work full-time before marriage, but unusual after marriage and certainly rare before the youngest child was under age 8 or 9. If parents had the intention of having more children if their finances improved (an eminently logical course), then later marriage in this type economy would facilitate having a larger family, hence the equation of later marriage = more children (higher fertility).

Even where money could not be saved we might see a violation of the regulatory theory, and *late marriage* did not necessarily entail *lower fertility*. The pre-Industrial economic situation was such that people sometimes saved money only with great difficulty, and the focus lay on what one earned at the present time, and what one could obtain from inheritance and borrowing. Further, if it was the people's custom to set aside a certain fixed amount of money per child, then wherever there was no significant difference in the amount of wealth that couples would have at the beginning of marriage, whatever the age of marriage, then there would be no difference in the number of children one eventually had. If inheritance of net worth from parents, or attaining a dowry was *not* a factor, then marrying late or early in these conditions made little difference. Creating a good current income basis for a household was the only important issue, but this income could only cover present expenses and little would be left over for savings. The financial position of a man marrying at 22 could only be a little worse than one marrying at 28, since the latter could have not added that much to his finances. In this case, marrying later does not mean marrying wealthier. Hence, if the early marrying couple and the late marrying couple each had saved little or no money, and each planned to set aside the same amount of money for the raising and care of each child, then both couples would have the same number of children, if nature allowed them this. The fertility rate in either case would be roughly the same, as the financial position and the amount that could be spent on each child would be little different. We would, therefore, see no correlation of any kind between age of marriage and fertility.

Because of situations like the ones above, the fertility governor or regulatory theory has come under criticism as not being applicable anywhere except the well-documented and well-studied country of England.[40] It appears that, in reality, the theory is generally applicable, but with notable exceptions. Apparent contradictions might be explained by one or more models, which incorporate personal, economic and cultural factors. Thus, there is no doubt that the interaction of employment, savings, living standards, inheritance and availability of marriage partners varied from one region to another, often due to exogenous factors, e.g. economic conditions. However, even when the end results are different between regions, based on an examination of evidence, one could conclude that the reasoning processes that people used were essentially the same, when microsocial aspects such as *personal ambitions, emotions, and family structure* were taken into account.

Using the foregoing as a guide, let us now look at the logic behind an interesting set of early 19th century customs as they existed in Nanterre, a town near Paris.[41] Firstly, the area's very high rate of return from the land made it possible for even small plots to produce an adequate living. Secondly, the fact that some of the children in a family could settle into work outside of agriculture reduced the likelihood of inordinate population pressure on the land. Further, due to the nature and demands of agriculture and wine growing, Nanterre did not ordinarily have resident servants who worked the land, but day labourers who worked whenever there was a need for outside assistance. Because of this practise, children originally helped out on the farm, and then after marriage, they left the household, and wage labour was brought in. This economic circumstance, where men and women could 'freelance' as labourers, and where farmers did not have to depend on a family for production, produced opportunities for independent living, resulting in a fairly large number of households being occupied by single adults: Bachelors, widows and widowers, with or without children. Nearly two-thirds of the households in Nanterre were nuclear, but some 23% were solitaires. Many unmarried men could live as boarders, and about 5% of the nuclear households had boarders living with them, usually because they produced significant income. These arrangements *lessened* the pressure to marry.

If people had a desire to marry, an extensive kinship system facilitated the securement of a marriage partner, because farmers lived in areas where neighbours were often relatives. People in this social climate evidently felt confidant enough in their future that it became common for parents and children to reach an agreement known formally as a *demission de biens*, where the parents would retire early, giving land to all their children in return for a life income. This allowed the children *to marry without having to wait for an inheritance*. Further, facilitating marriage for the children of farmers was the practise of giving some land to children upon their wedding, and the practise of furnishing a father's dowry. Daughters could save money in anticipation of marriage by working as laun-

dresses or seamstresses. Artisans, on the other hand, who came to
Nanterre and so had to take the time to establish themselves, married later. They had fewer family members to draw upon for assistance, as can be seen in the fact that often they had friends, instead
of relatives, witness their weddings. This social class also had fewer
financial resources, and so dowries were less common.

Not surprisingly, farmers' marriages were both socially and
geographically endogamous; most people wed those in the same
trade or occupation as themselves or their fathers'. Whereas the
marriage practises of Nanterre were not particularly common elsewhere, the desirability of marrying someone from the same background as onself reflected a very common theme. For example,
socially prestigious farmers/wine growers' daughters often would
marry sons from the same trade, although there was a tendency for
daughters to marry sons from other trades. The social situation did
not remain static, and following changes in the economic structure,
artisans grew in status and become numerous after 1820. Although
other trades were generally endogamous and people preferred
similarity, there was a 'pull' to marry into the largest and most
lucrative occupations. Exogenous factors freed people to make
decisions about their adult life and marriage without having to
worry about future obligations, family duty to work on a farm, or
possible financial problems due to overly large families, early marriage or waiting for an inheritance, especially for younger sons.
Therefore, economics to a significant extent determined the nature
of family relations, in at least this part of France.

However, in the south and the more remote areas of France, a
very different culture applied, but one that was still based on exogenous variables.[42] To put it succinctly, as the economy weakened,
so did family relationships; the culture allowed the external forces
to impact logic and reasoning, and thus ideals foundered. Without
overgeneralising, we can say that people essentially lived in a
closed, rather suspicious world, where people erected successive

barriers around themselves as a form of protection. Living in small villages, farmers and their families were distrustful and sometimes hostile to outsiders. Within the household, fathers held nearly total control, with wives in secondary position and children even further subordinated. Families rarely had cordial relations with one another, even though they frequently had to work with one another. Children were used as farm labourers, and if a child worked somewhere else, he would be expected to give over his earnings to his family. We also see that respect for traditional parental functions was declining, with schools taking over many child-rearing tasks, including the daily supervision and education of children. Men and women were warned to refrain as much as possible from giving money and land to their children, because this would only put parents at the mercy of their offspring. Although families were usually restrained in speech, parents often did not hide their dislike for their own children, and parents in turn were also derided and maltreated, especially in old age. A lack of faith between parents and children was matched by a distrust between the sexes, which began in childhood, and then continued into adulthood; men became indifferent to women, thinking that they were responsible for man's downfall. Many regions had high rates of celibacy, which might partly explain the denigration of women. By the end of the 19th century, fertility was dropping considerably, not only because of celibacy, but also because married couples were limiting fertility. How else could couples save themselves from the potentially disastrous fate of raising children, only to have them selfishly and spitefully abandon them in old age for better opportunities elsewhere?

Hence, in this strained situation, we see *division* and *segmentation*. It was 'need and greed' that kept families together, not mutual desire, affection, or moral compunction. Companionate relationships were indeed difficult to come by, and people spent more time using psychological devices to distance themselves from each another, than pulling themselves toward one another. A simple emotional device could be utilised in many different situations: If one devalues what one really desires, then one can convince oneself that one does not want it that badly. The social modality in the southern French countryside, especially when distilled into the simplified form as seen above, is manifestly contradictory. Why would parents maltreat their children if they expected to depend on them in old age? Were they surprised when their own children treated them like animals when they were treated the same way? Why would families live together with animosity and rancour when they needed each other for support? The only rational answer is that *people no longer thought they were able to obtain what they wanted from the family, and thus disparaged it*. What we see is a case of a transient culture, where the insufficiency and despair of the 19th century created a crisis situation of mutual vindictiveness. The adage that the 'worst of times brings out the best in people' is fanciful at best, and here we see good evidence of insuperable human frailty. When put into difficult circumstances, instead of becoming even more promotive of honour, devotion, and respect, people degenerate to pettiness, aloofness, and generalisations, in essence causing them and the family to self-destruct. Perhaps the meanness stemmed from the realisation that a culture and a way of life were about to pass into history.

In times of peril, individuals, without training or prior experience, tend to over-control their personal environment. An attempt was made to achieve intermediate goals against the strong crosswinds of financial expediency, but instead of using subtle movements that allow the various forces to fall into an equilibrium, many used their options rashly and crudely, making attaining a steady course a hopeless undertaking. In such a challenging scenario, with the knowledge always in mind of the dangerous consequences that come from error, one desires clear results quickly, with any delay being disturbing. One could gain control of even very difficult situations by simply allowing the various mechanisms to 'settle down' after initiating some kind of action. Raising children and dealing with a family in difficult material circumstances is sure to provoke people to take harsh measures for rapid, certain results, but by doing so, they sow the seeds of enmity that will come back to haunt them.

Reasons for this kind of social turmoil are not impossible to find. A major contributor to the problems that families faced might have been one component of the Code Napoléon (1804), which forced landowners to divide their property *equally among heirs*. This made it difficult for farmers to resist the temptation to limit births so that the land would not be split up, causing hardship for future generations, and destroying family power. Where property ownership was common, birthrates indeed fell. However, as many peasants did not own the land they farmed, the laws concerning inheritance had limited applicability, although at the time, this reason was commonly assumed. More relevant, and perhaps more troubling, a factor, which explains declining birthrates, was an economic environment where children no longer had the monetary and pragmatic value they once did. Here, contraception, continence and late marriage combined to restrain fertility.

Still, the most important reason for the indigence of the peasantry might have been due to the fruits of government corruption and incompetence, namely high taxes and rents. They struggled to survive under onerous burdens over which they had little control. Our sympathy for the peasants is, however, tempered by the knowledge that their plight was to some significant extent self-imposed as well. As in indication of major lapses in logic, we can cite the fact that these country people, despite being regarded as simple in tastes, would often sell their best agricultural products in order to buy items that might be considered frivolous.[43] By the late 19th century, most people in France had many options as to where they could work, what kind of work they could do, what productivity measures they could implement, how and what they could sell, and what they could buy. Consequently, as personal choice played a role in determining quality of life, so did it, at the very least, *indirectly* affect marriage timing, family size and family structure.

The south of France was not alone in its economic deprivation, nor in its reaction to it. Analysis of conditions in contemporaneous Ireland, although very different in history and politics, demonstrates that the spirit of the people described above, far from being characterised as merely 'French', could quite justifiably be called 'European'. Before the Famine, in many parts of Ireland land was subdivided and given to sons, as families relied on the labour of family members. Therefore, what was the product of *law* in France, was the product of *folk culture* in Ireland. Subsistence on these smaller holdings would not have been possible, however, without grain prices rising and the viability of cottage industries. Yet, after the Famine the situation changed dramatically. The former land practises were no longer valid, and the room for error was perceived as being far smaller; at that time, the cultural spirit became more visible and easily dissected. Land came to be poorly managed and yield declined, with the result that culture now demanded that inheritance be impartible. For this state of affairs, many blamed the landlords, the English and the Protestants, but few blamed the peasants themselves who were evidently chiefly responsible. As a result of this factional fighting and continuing age-old rivalries in the community, people became reluctant to hire outside help, instead they used more dependable family labour.

Thus, when land inheritance and dowries did not materialise, the basis of married life was withdrawn, and many never married. Those who did marry, did so with money as a prime consideration, although many marriages were arranged without much consent from the prospective bride. These changes exerted a major toll on relations within the household, causing dangerous centripetal forces to arise within the family. Women were frequently treated as units of production in loveless relationships, and often married considerably older men. In fact, it became common by the turn of the 20th century that half of married women were more than 10 years younger than their spouses. As parents did not wish to yield control and delegate authority in domestic matters to children, resentment tainted ordinary relationships, and even firstborn sons were kept in subordinate positions for many years into adulthood.

We can see here underlying dynamics, the most important of which, for our purposes, is the emphasis that was given to the concept of an absolute minimal standard of living, that is, people put material independence over that of familial affection and sacrifice. As a result, the standard of living for each family member would *not* change, in relation to modifications in household size. In a society that was as materially minded as post-Famine Ireland, a person's 'worth' was based on his economic 'worth'.

For example, the main reason, we suspect, why the youngest sons were most condescendingly treated, is because they threatened to make it impossible for everyone to get their legitimate 'slice of the pie', a portion that was theirs by 'right'. These individuals often threw the family into financial disarray, but they managed, however, to form close alliances with their mothers, who, probably because of their lower productivity during pregnancy, found themselves similarly deprecated. Not surprisingly, selfishness, distrust and feelings of inferiority abounded, but for those who wished a better life there were few options, as few urban areas required labour and servant status would bring even further disrepute. Thus, many who did not inherit land escaped to America, in the process breaking up families and creating yet more animosity and envy among those who remained.

People had to react in decisive ways to crises, and so marriage standards were raised, with the result that many men and women did not find each other sufficiently aesthetically, economically or romantically attractive. Men wanted to raise themselves above the ignominy of labourers and neglected sons. The common acceptance of the saying that 'the lucky man waits for prosperity', that is, waits for the propitious union with a well-to-do woman, resulted in fairly high rates of permanent celibacy in this period. About 25% of women never married in the period after the Famine, and the ones who did evidently had some difficulty in maintaining their rights and prerogatives in the matter of their prospective spouse. Some women went to work overseas in order to obtain enough money to lure prospective bridegrooms. In a situation similar to that in certain parts of France, the money would be used to buy frivolous items, such as better clothing and jewellery, creating the distinct impression of some wealth,[44] indicating that appearances rather than real merit had already become the focus of courtship. Irish marriage rates and birth rates did not significantly change since 1864, when records began to be kept, until the 1960s. Other countries' rates declined over this period, eventually catching up with the trend in Irish births, whereas Ireland's marriage rates are still considerably lower than that of other nations. Because of the above factors, Ireland was a 'modern' nation before any other in Europe,[45] and its microsocial patterns challenge Hajnal's theories about economic conditions being invariably linked to marriage patterns.

Promoters of the theory of economic pragmatism ignore the importance of other *incentives* to wed, as marriage is a whole 'package' of considerations, including appearance, personality, and deportment. Pre-existing compatibility between future spouses, at least in the area of manners, was now an issue. No matter how hard they tried to be 'pragmatic', the Irish could not countenance marrying a person still burdened with the 'rustic image'. In addition, incentives to not marry could be found by this time, such as support from siblings, surrogate heirs and the government.[46] It is probably from this period that many unfavourable proverbs were created, such as, 'beat a woman with a hammer and you'll have gold', 'it is difficult to trust a woman', 'there's only one thing in the world better than a good wife—no wife.' Some of these reflect the negativistic thinking of the English, French and other cultures, but undoubtedly they had a poignant ring in Ireland.

Ireland was typical of all other pre-modern nations in depending on land as wealth, forestalling marriage when it was unavailable. But it was different from other countries in not having industry as compensation for high population density, and very unwise subdivision practises. The lack of cooperation between family members, as well as the materialism, might have been influenced by a poor economy, and so might occur anywhere in Europe, under similar circumstances. However, microsocial factors might alter the extent of the turmoil. In Ireland, this was a recipe for disaster: The mixture of early marriage age, and the practise of partible inheritance, produced many heirs with small plots of land, who found themselves backward and isolated in a country with sluggish industrial growth. The result was enormous starvation when the land was pushed finally past its limit to produce. In the aftermath of the Famine, the family situation changed but apparently for the worse, where whatever civility was left was extinguished by the struggle for the remaining resources. It is true that famine can happen anywhere, and people can lose their heads in desperation, but the Famine in Ireland was much more disruptive due to the absence of *economic collaboration, industriousness, and progressivity*, psychological conditions that might be peculiarly Irish. Even as patriots might have us believe otherwise, characterisations of a people must also carry temporal limits, and so our observation is appropriate for the people living on the island before the mid-1800s, but perhaps not those living there in the present day.

Compared to the peasantry of France and Ireland, in social structure and lifestyle the nobility of Southwest Germany were very different indeed. Nevertheless, they had a similar, albeit more consistent, long-term reaction to economic forces, indicating a logic that was more resistant to external forces. The evidence, as presented in Hurwich (1993), shows that people did not divide estates among offspring during economic downturns mainly to preserve their prestigious way of life, and as a result, hardly half of the sons and daughters born in the 15th century married. Most of the unmarried sons, and nearly all the unmarried daughters entered the Church, this being especially true for lower-ranking noble families. Higher-ranking families placed sons in military careers.

This intriguing pattern was similar in other Catholic parts of Europe: Florence before 1700, Milan before 1750, Toulouse before 1760. Remarkably, half the sons and half the daughters of 17th century French dukes and peers did not marry. When Protestantism became the established religion in various regions, daughters were more likely to marry, one reason being that there were no convents in which to place them. However, in other Protestant parts of Europe, the older ways persisted, such as the Protestant part of Geneva, where a quarter of sons and daughters did not marry.

The reason why land was not divided among heirs rests primarily upon economics. In general, the eldest son did not necessarily inherit, and although there is a long-standing tradition for *all* brothers to inherit, this was done only when economic circumstances allowed. In the 15th century, during a period of agricultural depression, and fewer options in secular careers, land division was avoided and more of the nobility's offspring entered the ranks of the Church. Conversely, the period of the 16th century and the early 17th century brought forth an expanding economy in agriculture and better occupational opportunities, with a concomitant policy amongst the nobility of subdividing estates. In this situation, fewer children remained unmarried, and fewer entered the clergy. By the late 17th century, noblemen again refrained from dividing estates, a tendency that was an outgrowth of the effect of the Thirty Years' War on grain and land prices, as well as on tenant income. Again, a larger proportion of children remained unmarried, although this effect was more pronounced for females and in general was not nearly at the levels seen in the period before the 16th century. In spite of dour financial circumstances, the more favourable marital outcome occurred as a result of men being able to engage in alternate occupations, and make honourable lives for themselves.

Thus, economic and demographic upheavals leave deep marks on people, who revise their outlook and priorities according to the realities at hand. These factors affected German proverbs, such as 'he who marries does well, but he who does not marry does better', or 'marriage is both heaven and hell'. They had a suspect view of marriage, but without the aspersions, or even misogyny of some other European cultures. The negative experiences of Germany in the Thirty Years War, and its growing pains as a nation might have reflected adversely on many households. The unfortunate dispute between the social ideal of equanimity (all brothers inheriting), and of economic reality (only the eldest inherited in difficult times), made many cast a stern eye on marriage perhaps as *psychological protection* against the heartbreak of not being in a position to inherit. The denial of marriage to a man or woman who was never attracted to it in the first place is no great hardship.

The invisible hand of fiscalism that pulled or pushed people into marriage in Europe, extended to regions more than three centuries and a continent away. People are indeed slow to transition into new lifestyles, and no matter where they lived, those raised within the culture of an agricultural community would as their forbears still consider land, and not only money, as necessary for marriage. The self-sufficiency of a farm—its independence —has an enduring appeal even today. This is why we notice that whites who resided in the rural southern United States in the early 20th century would delay marriage, if farmland was expensive, and jobs outside of agriculture (i.e. manufacturing) were available.[47] As in Europe, land was king, and the difficulty in obtaining it significantly affected the timing of a man's entry into family life. In the urban environment, where land for most people was an irrelevant factor, income became the main focus. Men working in factories could

often only find a meagre basis for a living, with marriage a distant
aim. Sometimes, however, the money from jobs in industry might
be good enough to maintain a household, but country people living
in the cities would still see this strategy, based as it was on nothing
more than 'paper money', as bound for failure.

Only if the rustic emigrants to the cities dispensed with their
belief in older traditions, could they utilise the savings from their
work, and marry early. This would, in essence, also nullify the
influence of inheritance practices on marriage.[48] Such newfound
freedom was indeed desirable and liberating, but it was tempered
by the knowledge that modern city life did not offer the safety of
family and land that existed in the 'backward' countryside. We see
that people in every country and situation had a definite personal
idea of the 'proper' *standard of living*, and they could not easily
envision a viable marriage that did not attain it.

Clearly, the avoidance of segmentation in the family or community was paramount, and we would like to know what was done
to achieve this end. Although the private, innermost thoughts of
most people on the matters of intimacy, companionship, and marriage have not been preserved, some indicators are available that
reveal such mental processes. One such source of evidence is the
proceedings of marriage courts, which contain the views of ordinary people and persons in authority on customs and contracts. We
have a rare instance of reliable data from the parish of Neuchâtel,
in Switzerland, where we can study the changes in procedures.[49]
Cases where one party wished to annul a marriage were brought
before a special court. In the period from the mid-16th century to
the mid-17th century, promises of marriage were binding if made
by persons at the age 20 or older and in front of two or more wit-
nesses. The marriage contract and the agreement to marry were
allowed to stand; whether the couple loved each other was not a
pertinent concern. By the 18th century, the emphasis moved from
a *strict application of vows* to a more *flexible approach* that took into

account *emotional and psychological compatibility*. This is an attitudinal shift of great significance. All of the parties concerned had to be assured that the couple really wanted to live with each other; even if promises were made, they were not considered binding unless the woman was pregnant, in which case the interests of the child overrode the interests of the parents.

It would appear that their legal strategy of maintaining traditional marriage was working, since the illegitimacy rate for Neuchâtel remained low (under 5%). Nonetheless, the increase in premarital pregnancies might have been considered alarming, as it indicated a breakdown in morality was occurring. No doubt justices felt compelled to declare a 'marriage contract' between a man and pregnant woman as valid, even if it did thwart the aim of a 'perfect' society built on a freely established, congruent households. The conditions in Switzerland was probably part of a larger pattern; although we do not have figures for premarital pregnancy in that country, we know that there was a large increase in such pregnancies in other parts of Europe, from the mid-18th century, to the early 19th century. For example, we cite the percent of premarital conceptions (births within 8 months of marriage) from the period before 1750, to the period around 1820: Germany, 13% to 24%, France, 6% to 13%, England, 20% to 35%.[50] Such conceptions were a 'warning sign', and legal institutions in many nations helped to avoid illegitimate births by forcing single pregnant women to marry. Thus, illegitimacy rates increased relatively little in certain nations, such as England, Spain and France, but they were more problematic in Germany, especially in certain regions. Bavarian rates increased from about 3% in the mid-18th century, to about 15% a century later. Other parts of Germany also experienced large increases, from at least 1700, and peaking around 1850.[51]

Switzerland experienced changes in fertility patterns to a lesser extent than Germany, but the changes were still disturbing enough to instigate a change in juridical theory on marriage customs and practise. Persons in authority, charged with safeguarding not only traditions but the family, realised that people were becoming less serious in contracting a marriage, and such figures wanted to be confident that married life would remain viable. The same frivolity that attended the decision to marry also undermined other important behaviours, arrangements, and responsibilities.

It seems that Swiss officials understood the changing morality, as intervention *preceded* the change in fertility and sexual attitudes. Officials often have a higher vantage point that gives them a better perspective on what is 'brewing' in the population. However, it would have been a superior strategy to insist on the validity of the marriage contract, as a warning to people not to enter engagement without giving careful thought to the feasibility of the relationship.

Thus, the traditional structures of marriage should have been preserved, as they functioned well within the cultural spheres of Europe. The insincerity, and uncertainty, behind the vows of marriage would have disappeared, when people understood the dire consequences that awaited the careless promise, but this could only have occurred during the period when the palpable virtues of devotion and integrity were still etched in living memory.

The evidence indicates that in the early Industrial period, the relationship between the outer spheres of society and the inner sphere of family life changed. The individual felt more disconnected from various macrosocial factors, instead pursuing his private goals without consulting tradition. Earlier, the demands of the economy were not overly burdensome, and people could adjust at a 'local' level. But in later periods, due to interference by governments and business, challenges to family structure occurred for which tradition had no remedy. Over time, certain traditional concepts were opposed and discarded, bringing divisions in society that threatened intimacy. As a result, the changes in friendship, courtship, and marriage practises provoked an ideal-negating subjectivity and inflexibility that continues to evolve even today.

Chapter 7

Conclusions

*E*veryone must cope with two powerful forces that strive for recognition in human affairs, that of love and independence. By marrying, people make the major choice to forego some of their independence, in order to achieve greater happiness by sharing all aspects of their life with another person. The personal freedom that is lost is offset, to a large extent, by the intimacy that is gained.

Yet, this decision has complicated consequences. We have examined the organic development of relationships, wherein people struggle to balance the two ideals of love and independence. We have, in particular, attempted to determine the nature, or essence, of each of these ideals. One can understand that these are not esoteric areas, but comprehensible concepts if one acknowledges that achieving both ideals requires determination and sacrifice. In the case of love, there must be virtue, and in the case of independence, there must be self-sufficiency. We can say that both are related, by observing that ultimately love is attained through effectiveness, and independence is achieved through efficiency. The combination of the *apotheosis* of each produces, by the standards of European culture, the perfect individual.

This is why modern people, despite utilising much of their intellectual and emotional energies for the purpose of increasing their income and career status, still hold for themselves, as an *ultimate goal,* the achievement of a companionate relationship. The individual might not admit it anyone else, but he still strives for the *social perfection* that his ancestors sought. By enacting moral and ethical principles, it is possible to marry and still retain a great deal of independence; if two people can find positive ways to understand and support one another, then independence does not have to be entirely sacrificed. Indeed, both spouses become stronger than before. Within this framework love can truly be liberated, and this is, after all, the great goal of all intelligent, compassionate people.

The rewards bestowed by wisdom, through a careful observance of the laws of human nature, have not diminished over time; rather, what has diminished is the proportion of the public who possess such genuine wisdom. There is, in the various historical documents, undeniable evidence of ordinary persons placing great emphasis on obtaining the time, money, and other resources to find a suitable marriage partner, in order to establish a viable household of their own. The formation of an independent household was a watershed event in the lives of most people. When resources could not be attained, due to poor employment prospects, little or no inheritance, or rising prices, people would then delay marriage. This did not mean that they did not wish to attain the ideal of love, but that it was put aside by pragmatic circumstances.

But lapses in judgement began to occur as the economy faltered. When people were prevented from marrying as a consequence of recession, then family members often became hostile, accusing one another, probably unfairly, of being at fault for this hindrance. This acted to destroy the bonds that might have been used as *substitutes* for the marital bond. Where a son or daughter might have obtained a satisfying emotional relationship from a father or mother, instead of a spouse, this possibility was destroyed by arguments over money, inheritance, land-sharing, and so on.

We see in these events the basis for the transformation of attitudes towards marriage, from one where economic considerations were a high priority in people's minds, *co-existing* with their emotional needs for companionship, to one where financial aspects are retained, but the emotional aspect is neglected, now looming like a tiger ready to pounce. Where before the couple could *grow with one another* into a mutual loving relationship, now the husband and wife often develop in different directions.

In the worst case scenario, the uniqueness of intimate companionship is lost. When the restrictions on marriage began to be lifted in the 18th century, due to conflicts between the calls of the new economy and the exigencies of married life, the emphasis shifted from marriage as a shelter of psychological and emotional deepening, to a materialistic venue where the fatuities of earlier life could continue, but now with certain added conveniences: Two individuals share, albeit guardedly, a house, food, furniture and other sundries to their mutual economic benefit.

The fundamental, essential precepts of modern married life had been set by the late 19th century, and the traditional conceptions, so beneficial to generations of people, were unobtrusively passing away. This is a loss for Western society, as so much can be learned from these older conceptions. Yet, by carefully studying history and sociology, people today can re-establish the wisdom of the past and integrate it into their own lives, avoiding the pitfalls of modernity.

In our struggle to comprehend the world, modern society provides little support, and it is only from the past that we can gain insight, from our ancestors who built up reasonable rules and guidelines that allowed them to emerge contented and confident even from the darkness of the most perilous times. Love and freedom can indeed be attained in any period, not by foolishly accepting whatever contemporary society has to say on the subjects, but by absorbing the great ideas from all generations, regardless of whether they are fashionable or not. In such a way, through the study of societies and cultures, across space and time, the individual can enlighten his mind, enrich his spirit, and safeguard his progress through life, even when the nation in which he lives offers only the most inefficient and ineffective pathways.

Notes

1   In a survey of six European nations (The European, 21 -23 Jan, 1991), of 14 high-importance activity areas, the *family* came out first in every country, with, on average, 88% saying they have a 'very strong' attachment. *Freedom* came second at 86% on average, followed by *rights of man, equality, democracy, work, culture, solidarity, marriage, the nation, free enterprise, Europe, money* and, lastly, *religion*. Although the actual percentages varied from country to country, the ranks of values were not very different. Notice that freedom is immediately followed by three related concepts, thus emphasising the role of independence in the modern world. Yet, there is an incongruous distancing between *family* and *marriage*, demonstrating that society is confused about the true nature of both concepts.

   In a survey of young people, when both emotions and activities, such as love and freedom, were used as value areas, the connections varied, depending to a certain extent on social status and age (Sugarman 1980). *Happiness* was the most important characteristic for both polytechnic students and high school students. However, *freedom,* followed by *mature love,* were important for the former group, but an *exciting life, mature love, pleasure* and *true friendship* were all equal in importance after *happiness* for the latter group, with *freedom* only then appearing as a concern. Perhaps younger people see freedom as not an important question, since their actions are limited by parents and by law. College students would have more of a reason to value freedom since their potential for autonomy lies to a large extent in their hands. In any case, younger people value happiness most (when asked), and then love and freedom; older people value family (instead of love), then freedom, and associated concepts of equality and rights.

2 Eastern Europe, during its Communist period, still had significantly more people marrying young, and had lower divorce rates, than Western Europe. This has been changing over the last 20 years, as many of these nations attempt various forms of capitalism and democratic government.

3 In speaking of sets of traits, people, whether they know it or not, often make a keen distinction between gender and sex, with the nature of this distinction varying from one social segment to another. 'Gender' is a set of attributes that a person can possess; 'sex', however, is often considered to contain innate aspects. Thus, society can look at the physiology of a person, and deduce whether they are male or female, based on examination of physique, skin, hair, internal organs, external organs, blood and genetic material. Nevertheless, gender is more difficult to define, as this term is comprised of aspects that are relevant to a particular society. The universality of sex is beyond dispute, but many traits could not be considered truly 'masculine' or 'feminine' everywhere, and at all times.

In this work, when 'sex' is mentioned, it can be determined from the context whether it concerns sociology or biology, behaviour or physique. This differentiation is a more formal assignment, compared to the one we see in ordinary life. For example, a person who is distinctly physically 'female', might be 'male' in gender because most of her attributes and activities are likelier to occur in people who are distinctly physically 'male'.

4 The rule of similarity is of course not without exceptions, as observation reveals nature's constant encounters with diversity. Such variety in the wild can only be based on one

factor: Survival, both for the individual and the species. This multiplicity of engagements might be related to an instinctual need for reducing the chances of being victimised by predators by levelling out the probability of errors. In reproduction, the male of the species might take several females, possibly for reasons of avoiding inbreeding through genetic variation. Human beings also have an innate need for diversity, which has two manifestations, biological and intellectual.

5 Tambs & Moum 1992.

6 Uhl 1989.

7 Although the literature on family life is voluminous, there is astonishingly little on modern courtship practises. Research is particularly sparse on European and derived cultures, other than that of England, America, France or Spain. One does not know why there is this paucity of research. Perhaps courtship is too commonly thought of as a 'ritualised process', and since modern dating practises leading up to marriage lack formalism, 'courtship' is no longer perceived to exist. However, even if courtship is not highly structured, there is little doubt that the pre-marital social activities of the couple form a pattern. The absence of restrictions or guidelines on dating is part of this courtship pattern, and must be investigated.

8 Sporer 1999.

9 ibid.

10 Ibsen quoted in *Love's Comedy* (1862), the proverb: 'A friend married, is a friend lost.' Percy Bysshe Shelley lamented: 'When a man marries, dies or turns Hindu, his best friends hear no more of him.'

11 De Sanctis 1982.

12 In most crimes the perpetrator and victim know one another. For example, for the year 1990, in only 14% of

murder cases known to police was the perpetrator a stranger, and in 33%, he or she was an acquaintance or friend; in 35% of these cases, the relationship between victim and offender was not known (Flanagan & Maguire 1992, p 399, Table 3.140).

13 Mersmann 1986, p 185, p 191.

14 Feld 1991.

15 See for example K. Doheny, 'Desperately seeking . . . anyone; single people are going to unusual lengths to meet people. Can people blame them? These days it takes creativity to find the perfect partner,' *Los Angeles Times*, Nov 14, 1994.

16 Sprecher & McKinney 1987.

17 Quote from *The Maid of the Mill* (1765), by Isaac Bickerstaff (c. 1735-1787).

18 Rifkin & Timms 1985, p 18. We might also add the example of the French genius, Antoine Lavoisier. Not only did he and his brilliant wife, Marie Anne, enjoy an excellent professional collaboration, they also shared the greatest mutual love and affection. Lavoisier's intelligence and virtue did not, regrettably, save him from persecution by the Revolutionary regime, and he was executed in 1794 for treason.

19 As presented, for example, in Ozment (1986), Mersmann (1986), and Kermode & Kermode (1995; especially letters 3, 19, 23, 25, 34, 61, 192).

20 Germans of the 16th century were not reluctant about showing great devotion to their wives, to marriage, and to domestic life (Ozment 1983, p 65). And perhaps the most 'wintry' people of all, the Puritans, were hardly averse to praising emotional attachment, and deepest love and affection in marriage. 'Such marriages were commonplace among the Puritans. They were grounded in a union, not of this world, but of the world to come' (Adair 1982, p. 269).

21 Ozment (1983) makes this clear when he says that 'Several recent studies . . . argue that little genuine affection existed in the early modern family . . . for wives and children the traditional family was a kind of bondage that stifled self-realization' (p 2). Gillis (1997) maintains that many, if not most, concepts of marriage, sex, family, and children are of fairly recent invention, since they evidently incorporate 'civilised', and therefore non-traditional, views which are empathetic of personal rights.

22 Burguière 1987.

23 The top five reasons as to why people would divorce are: Infidelity, loss of affection, emotional problems, financial problems, physical abuse. Relatively few will escape experiencing these predicaments, as less than 60% of contemporary couples will still be together after 20 years of marriage (Chadwick & Heaton 1992, C1-3., p 86; C3-5., p 97). It would appear that although modern people claim that marriage is only based on love, finances are also of great concern, no doubt as they were in the past.

It is ironic that people of the present day think that their ancestors laboured in loveless, stifling marriages, racked by financial woes, when ironically they *themselves* suffer from precisely this fate. Is this, perhaps, an example of a type of psychological projection?

24 Admittedly, it is difficult to determine the parameters of the everyday life in the traditional period. People undoubtedly made their most intimate thoughts known in their letters, but few of these are published. Instead, scholars have sought to bring forward into public view supposedly more interesting matters relating to politics, government, economics, law and so forth. But what could be more important than human relations of the most spiritual kind? No doubt there are thousands of letters and diaries, from

people of all classes, revealing varied, deep emotional senti-
ments, gathering dust in archives. Until scholars have the
resources, and see the necessity, for exhuming them, we
must do with what we have. What is clear, however, is that
when people speak of affection, and give it a central place
in their personal writings, they do not see it as curious or
unusual, or something that needs to be hidden because
decent people would find it inappropriate. Further, if we
consider the writers to be typical with respect to reflecting
the tastes and standards of the time, we are then able to
make a reasonable estimate of contemporary customs.

25 For examples, see Blum 1974.

26 We can see similar problems that anthropologists face in
their observations of primitive peoples. For example, Mar-
garet Mead's observations of the Samoan people (as described and critiqued in Torrey 1992, pp 72-74) have been
rendered dubious by the work of later investigators, who
found a culture quite different from the one she describes.
It would appear that Mead's bullying tactics and difficulty
with the language, as well as the natives' purposely inaccu-
rate statements (made often as 'jokes'), all yielded a highly
artificial view of their society, which was then further pro-
cessed through a disposition of mind which favoured those
ideas that fit in with a personal and political agenda. The
resulting 'culture' was as mythical as anything the Samoans
themselves could have invented.

27 There is little doubt that contemporary observers could be
confused or mistaken, and from this we find apparent contradictions. For example, whereas early to mid-19th century
observers characterised the peasantry of southern France
as poorly dressed, vulgar, barely civilised, brutal, hardly
better than animals (Weber 1976, p. 4), early 17th century
Languedoc and Provence were found to contain villages

and towns where women dressed in many different materials and colours; in the latter case, there was so much variety that some observers found it excessive (Kettering 1978,
p 14-15). Further, depictions of peasants in various Books
of Hours of the 15th century show the French people as
basically well-fed, well-dressed, in colourful, perhaps
nearly 'bourgeois' clothing. Are these differences a reflection of changes over time, are they the result of faulty observation, or are they simply a result of prejudices that do
not allow the acceptance of the 'prosperous peasant' concept? There is no doubt that many farm families were very
poor, but what about a well-to-do rustic? Is that beyond
belief? It would appear that in Europe, there has almost
always existed a standard-of-living scale with many grada-
tions, not only amongst town-dwellers, but also amongst
the country people. Authors writing about the cultures of
their own time not infrequently gave widely different as-
sessments of living conditions of the same land, as for example in the cases of early 19th century England, France,
Poland, Hungary and Romania.

28 Using the criteria discussed, we find that the statistics derived from Flinn (1981), which provides parish data from
different regions of different nations (England, France,
Germany, Scandinavia, Switzerland), show, in general,
great similarity in the areas of marriage age, illegitimate
births, and premarital conceptions, but *not so with age-
specific fertility, birth intervals, and age of birth of last child.*
When it comes to testing for the existence of deviation from
the norm, and therefore *free choice,* we do find positive
evidence in virtually all recorded life areas, except for illegitimacy. Economic expediency certainly might explain
some, or most, of the variation. We are constrained, however, from being more certain about this, since we do not

know the precise economic conditions that applied in these diverse areas. Furthermore, when it comes to something like premarital conceptions (and by connection, ideas about courtship, fondness, and affection), economics does not seem particularly relevant, and thus individual choice might be quite germane as an explanatory mechanism.

29 Chapter IX, Twenty-Fourth Session; Schroeder 1978, p 189.

30 Roman Catholic Church 1908, p 401.

31 Flinn 1981, pp 118-123. France and Germany, but not England, were below 20% for premarital conceptions.

32 Wrigley 1987, Figure 9.5, pp 232-233.

33 Weber 1976, p 18. This correlation disappeared by 1876, however, perhaps due to less explicit concern about the impact of economics on satisfaction in married life.

34 Hajnal 1965.

35 Alter 1991. The main challenges revolve around the inability to explain why late marriage persisted so long in the cities, when economic opportunities facilitating early marriage were present. Indeed, due to economic growth and urbanisation throughout Europe, there should have been an overall *lowering* of marriage age in the 19th century.

36 Kuklo 1991.

37 Kuklo 1991. The figures were calculated after those of 'unknown' marital status were removed.

38 Wrigley 1987, pp 281-283. In France, many men would marry women older than themselves as a way of limiting fertility, including middle-age widows (Weber 1976, p 185). Aphorisms about this were contradictory, showing to a certain extent the ambiguity that surrounded the issue; popular sayings put into relief pragmatic concerns, against the background of emotional needs.

39 Wrigley 1987, p 257.

40 Spagnoli 1983.

41 Segalen 1991.

42 See Weber 1976, pp 167-191.

43 Weber 1976, pp 134-135.

44 Miller 1985, pp 54-60, pp 402-409.

45 Mitchell 1975.

46 Guinnane 1991.

47 Landale & Tolnay 1991.

48 Industrialisation, regardless of its net effect on the economy, might have encouraged impartible inheritance. As men could find work in the town and cities, parents did not have to provide a living to children, and land therefore did not have to be shared. This would have intensified the practice of restricting the inheritance of land to one only son, forcing younger or non-inheriting sons to leave.

49 Watt 1988. There is evidence that the marriage Courts in certain regions showed flexibility and discretion in these matters even before the 18th century. Johann Christian Bach (1645-1694), an ancestor to Johann Sebastian Bach, worked as a court musician to Count Ludwig Günther at Arnstadt. He was brought before the Consistory for breach of marriage promise. The Court initially decided that he had to marry the woman in question, but he refused to accept their decision, stating that he had no love for her. The case went on for more than two years, before the Court found in his favour (see Williams CF, 1900, *Bach*, JM Dent & Co). Bach apparently did not suffer any penalty, fine, or social ostracism for his defiance. As defenders of a most sacred institution, these Courts had to show sensitivity to the complexities of human disposition and personality on the one hand, and a firmness in enforcing state and customary laws on the other.

50 Flinn 1981, Table 6, pp 121-123.

51 Shorter 1980, pp 113-120.

References

Adair J, 1982, *Founding Fathers, The Puritans in England and America*, J.M. Dent & Sons, Ltd, London.

Alter G, 1991, New perspectives on European marriage in the nineteenth century, *Journal of Family History*, Jan 16(1), 1-5.

Blum J., 1974, The condition of the European peasantry on the eve of emancipation, *Journal of Modern History*, Sep 46, 395-424.

Burguière A., 1987, The formation of the couple, *Journal of Family History*, Jan-Jul 12(1-3), 39-53.

Chadwick B.A., Heaton T.B., 1992, eds, *Statistical Handbook on the American Family*, Oryx Press, Phoenix.

De Sanctis P., 1982, [Spells, love potions and other tricks: Notes on the peasant woman and her marital destiny], *Rassegna Italiana di Sociologia*, Apr-Jun 23(2), 271-289.

Feld S.L., 1991, Why your friends have more friends than you do, *American Journal of Sociology*, May 96(6), 1464-1477.

Flanagan TJ, Maguire K, 1992, eds. *Sourcebook of Criminal Justice Statistics 1991*, U. S. Department of Justice, Bureau of Justice Statistics, Washington, DC.

Flinn, M.W., 1981, *The European Demographic System, 1500-1820*, Johns Hopkins University Press, Baltimore, MD.

Gillis, J.R., 1997, *A World of Their Own Making*, Harvard University Press, Cambridge.

Guinnane T., 1991, Re-thinking the Western European marriage pattern: The decision to marry in Ireland at the turn of the twentieth century, *Journal of Family History*, Jan 16(1), 47-64.

Hajnal J., 1965, European marriage patterns in persepctive, in *Population in History*, eds. D.V. Glass and D.E.C. Eversley, Edward Arnold, London, pp 101-146.

Hurwich J.J., 1993, Inheritance practices in early modern Germany, *Journal of Interdisciplinary History*, Spr 23(4), 699-718.

Kermode F., Kermode, A., 1995, *The Oxford Book of Letters*, Oxford University, Oxford.

Kettering S, 1978, *Judicial Politics and Urban Revolt in Seventeenth-Century France*, Princeton University Press, Princeton.

Kuklo C., 1991, Marriage in pre-industrial Warsaw in the light of demographic studies, *Journal of Family History*, 15(3), 239-259.

Landale N.S., Tolnay S.E., 1991, Group differences in economic opportunity and the timing of marriage: Blacks and whites in the rural South, 1910, *American Sociological Review*, Feb 56(1), 33-45.

Mersmann H., ed, 1986, *Letters of Mozart*, Dorset Press, New York.

Mieder, W., 1986, *The Prentice Hall Encyclopedia of World Proverbs*, Prentice-Hall, Englewood Cliffs, New Jersey.

Miller K.A., 1985, *Emigrants and Exiles*, Oxford University Press, Oxford.

Mitchell B.R., 1975, *European Historical Statistics, 1750-1970*, Columbia University Press, New York.

Orbuch T.L., Veroff J., Holmberg D., 1993, Becoming a married couple: The emergence of meaning in the first years of marriage, *Journal of Marriage and the Family*, Nov 55(4), 815-826.

Ozment S., 1983, *When Fathers Ruled: Family Life in Reformation Europe*, Harvard University Press, Cambridge.

Reher D.S., 1991, Marriage patterns in Spain, *Journal of Family History*, 16(1), 7-30.

Rifkin J., Timms C., 1985, *Heinrich Schütz*, pp 1-150 in *The New Grove North European Baroque Masters*, S. Sadie, ed, W.W. Norton & Company, New York.

Roman Catholic Church, 1983, *Code of Canon Law*, Latin-English Edition, Canon Law Society of America, Washington, DC.

Rotberg R.I., Rabb T.K., 1980, eds., *Marriage and Fertility, Studies in Interdiscplinary History*, Princeton University Press, Princeton.

Schroeder H.J., 1978, *Canons and Decrees of the Council of Trent*, English Translation, Tan Books and Publishers, Inc., Rockford, Illinois.

Segalen M., 1991, Mean age at marriage and kinship networks in a town under the influence of the metropolis: Nanterre, 1800-1850, *Journal of Family History*, 16(1), 65-78.

Shorter E, 1980, Illegitimacy, sexual revolution, and social change in modern Europe, in Rotberg & Rabb (1980), p 85-120.

Spagnoli P.G., 1983, Industrialization, proletarianization and marriage: A reconsideration, *Journal of Family History*, Fall 8(3), 230-247.

Sporer P.D., 1999, *The Effect of Economic, Educational, Personality, and Family Factors on the Propensity to Marry*. Unpublished paper.

Sporer P.D., 2010A, *The Dimensions of Companionship*, Quenstedt Press, Chester.

Sporer P.D., 2010B, *Equal but Different*, Quenstedt Press, Chester.

Sporer P.D., 2010C, *The Concept of Family*, Quenstedt Press, Chester.

Sprecher S., McKinney K., 1987, Barriers in the initiation of intimate heterosexual relationships and strategies of intervention, *Journal of Social Work and Human Sexuality*, Spr Sum 5(2), 97-110.

Sugarman L., 1980, Choice and values among students, *Educational Research*, Feb 22(2), 143-146.

Tambs K., Moum T., 1992, No large convergence during marriage for health, lifestyle, and personality in a large sample of Norwegian spouses, *Journal of Marriage and the Family*, 54(4), 957-971.

Torrey EF, 1992, *Freudian Fraud*, HarperCollins, New York.

Uhl S., 1989, Making the bed: Creating the home in Escalona, Andalusia, *Ethnology*, 1989, Apr 28(2), 151-166.

Watt J.R., 1988, Marriage contract disputes in early modern Neuchatel, 1547-1806, *Journal of Social History*, Fal 22(1), 129-148.

Weber E., 1976, *Peasants into Frenchmen, The Modernization of Rural France, 1870-1914*, Stanford University Press, Stanford, California.

Wrigley E.A., 1987, *People, Cities and Wealth*, Basil Blackwell, Oxford.

Index